Low-Calorie
Party
Cook Book

Low-Calorie Party Cook Book

Suzy Chapin

CHL CREATIVE HOME LIBRARY
IN ASSOCIATION WITH BETTER HOMES AND GARDENS
MEREDITH CORPORATION

About the Author

Suzy Chapin has been creating low-calorie recipes since 1965 when she became concerned about her mother's overweight problem. To help with her diet, Mrs. Chapin invented countless low-calorie dishes which were so tasty and filling that her mother lost—and has kept off—45 pounds. This collection of recipes eventually comprised Mrs. Chapin's first cookbook, THE ADJUSTABLE DIET COOKBOOK. Today, she cooks nothing but low-calorie food for both family and guests. Because she feels that even the fanciest dinner parties need not mean added pounds, she conceived all the delicious, low-calorie menus in LOW-CALORIE PARTY COOK BOOK. Besides writing books, cooking, and raising a family, Mrs. Chapin does needlepoint, swims regularly, and is President of the Elizabeth, New Jersey Gardening Club.

CHL Creative Home Library
© 1971 by Meredith Corporation, Des Moines, Iowa
SBN 696–30300–0
Library of Congress Number 70–168466
All rights reserved
Printed in the United States of America
Cover design: Ronald Gilbert
Photography: Thom de Santo

Credits
China: Josiah Wedgwood & Sons, New York, New York
Flowers and plants: Caronia & Corless Flowers, Inc., New York, New York
Glassware and plastics: Bonniers, New York, New York
Ukranian accessories: Surma Book & Music Company, New York, New York

Contents

Introduction

This is a cookbook that tells how to give lovely parties without fattening food. Parties are so much fun to give and to attend that it's too bad to hear people moan that too many parties mean too much weight gained. Think how satisfying it is to give a marvelous party and know that your guests aren't being overstuffed. When your guests find out (if you decide to tell them), they will be overjoyed. No fooling.

Just what is low-calorie entertaining, and how can we equate calorie-reduced foods with true hospitality? It somehow goes against the grain; traditional hospitality has always meant the lavishing of rich, abundant victuals on one's guests, treating them to all the openhanded generosity one can manage. But the new world and the demands of modern society require a new life style—an emphasis on quality, not quantity. Not everyone is thrilled at the sight of mountains of food. Panic can set in at the sight of a groaning board. *What can I possibly find to eat that won't send the scales sky-high tomorrow?* is the despairing dieter's first thought.

Of course, not everyone is on a diet. But stop and think how many people you know who are underweight. Not very many, I'm willing to bet. The hostess with real know-how will find a way to give a beautiful party without unbalancing anyone's caloric budget. She will keep the pleasure of savoring the delicious party food while paring calories as much as possible.

This is a menu book. Every party is planned from tempting first course through imaginative dessert, because it does no good to cut calories in the main dish and then blow the whole bit with a Double Fudge Nut Three Layer Cake. These menus have been planned as balanced meals. Textures and colors have also been considered. Smooth and crunchy, tart and sweet, light and dark—everything should be in contrast to its companions. How boring to have everything the same!

Of course no menu is entirely guestproof—I still remember a Sunday night soup supper which nearly gave me heart failure. The menu was simple: hearty vegetable soup, rolls, a fruit salad lavished with melons, strawberries, and pears, and a rum cream pie for dessert. One of the guests, a new acquaintance, announced as he seated himself, "I never eat soup." Unruffled, I served him anyway. Glancing at the salad, he went on, "I don't eat salad, either." I passed him a roll. Everyone talked. Time for dessert finally came. The rum pie was the most luscious, fattening, fabulous thing I have ever made (I don't make it anymore because it is *too* rich). One bite, and down went his fork. "There's liquor in this!" Speechless, I could only nod. At this point his wife hit him. Banged him right on the head! If she hadn't I think I would have. But that was long ago and we were very young. You see, no matter how you plan, things can sometimes go wrong.

The whole point of entertaining is to have a good time. If the hostess enjoys the party it's a sure thing the guests have fun, too. Planning menus ahead, marketing early and preparing much of the food the day before help make entertaining, and the enjoyment of the party, easy for the hostess. A well-stocked pantry, which today includes your freezer, makes spontaneous and impromptu gatherings possible. Several parties of this sort are described farther on in the book.

The choice of menu and the method of preparation hold the secret of successful calorie-reduced entertaining. Nothing is more important than these two things when you want to have a party that won't make anyone fat. If you are conscious of what makes some foods fattening and others not, why some cooking methods add calories and others subtract them, and how you can cut caloric corners without losing flavor, appearance and palatability, you can become a low-calorie gourmet hostess whose guests will rejoice at your table.

Today more and more people are interested in nutrition. In spite of this, many Americans are addicted to carbohydrates and fat. Protein is most important for good health, and can be found in fish, meat, eggs and milk. Translated into party food, this means we can plan delectable menus based on seafood, lean meats, poultry, eggs, fresh fruit and vegetables.

If you really don't know much about calories, invest a quarter in a government publication called "Calories and Weight," Home and Garden Bulletin No. 153, available from the Superintendent of Documents, U.S. Government Printing Office, Washington, D.C. 20402. It not only lists many foods with their calorie count, it also has a guide for estimating the sizes of various kinds of meat, with drawings and measurements. This is basic, good, accurate information.

Fish, chicken, veal and lamb all contain fewer calories than beef, with fish having the least. Butter, margarine and oil all contain roughly the same number of calories (a lot: 100 per tablespoon). Nevertheless, I still use real butter (or margarine) in most places, and real sugar, too. What is half a cup of butter divided among twelve people? Only two-thirds tablespoon, or 66⅔ calories per person! (When you see something called "diet margarine," remember that it got that way by having air beaten into it, along with some water. This is fine for spreading on your morning toast, or putting on asparagus—but it separates on heating, so you can't use it for cooking.) One teaspoon of sugar contains 18 calories, and a small amount of sugar has its place in the average good diet. (Sugar substitutes, since the cyclamate ban, have been unsatisfactory. If you are under doctor's orders to cut out sugar, you will have to experiment with the recipes, using whatever brand or type of substitute you find works best. The same thing applies to a salt-free diet.) Remember, this is not a diet book. This is a calorie-reduced book, designed to help you give more and better parties.

Many of the low-calorie foods are very high in elegance for parties—foods such as mushrooms, lobster, crabmeat, Rock Cornish hens, brook trout, salmon, pineapple and strawberries. A huge bowl of crisp, pink shrimp with a spicy tomato sauce can be the cornerstone of a buffet table. Thin slices of London Broil are a delicious source of protein. A dip based on calorie-reduced cottage cheese (90 calories a cup, just to give you a clue), whirred up in a blender with plenty of seasoning, and surrounded by a variety of raw vegetables, looks and tastes wonderful and won't add pounds. (When you realize that a cup of sour cream contains 480 calories, the low-calorie cottage-cheese dip comes on strong as a calorie saver.)

The menus have been planned with an eye on the availability of foods. It would be ridiculous to suggest fresh raspberries in February, although strawberries seem to be on hand almost all year round. Fresh seafood is not always easy to find inland, so I have suggested using frozen or canned, remarkably good nowadays—often frozen right on the fishing vessel.

What you save in not buying heavy cream you can spend on nonfattening goodies. The proprietor of one of the most elegant French restaurants in

New York's east fifties told me he no longer buys heavy cream for the chef. "Everyone is conscious of diet now," he said, "and won't order the rich food we used to make." You see? Everybody is doing it!

Of course, just buying low-calorie food is not the whole story. The method of cooking is what makes all the difference. Teflon-lined pans are the greatest help in cooking calorie-reduced food. With Teflon-lined skillets and saucepans you can make rich, smooth, scrumptious sauces and main dishes, using the barest minimum of butter or oil (sometimes even *none*). Teflon-lined molds for timbales, soufflés, charlottes and gelatin salads and desserts make it so easy to unmold these spectacular party dishes.

When you plan a party, the overall scene is important. The flowers, dishes, and serving pieces all reflect the kind of party you are having. Many times you will not need flowers for the tables. Consider using a beautiful collection of fresh greens in a French salad basket, as shown in the photograph opposite page 87, for your table decoration. Use a pile of shiny yellow lemons, or even a basket of eggs, on your informal table. Look through your collection of figurines or statuettes and use one of them as the focal point of a formal table. Butterflies, captured forever in blocks of lucite, can bring a summertime look to a wintry dinner. Take an hour and look through your treasured collection of "things"; see them with new eyes, and bring them forth for your guests to enjoy.

In your planning, always keep in mind the mechanics of entertaining. My table will hold only ten people comfortably, so I never have more than that number for a sit-down dinner. A buffet party is more successful if you have warming devices to keep the serving dishes at the right temperature while your guests serve themselves. Candle warmers can go under casseroles; chafing dishes and electric hot trays are all helpful. Set the food out in the logical serving order, with plates, silver, and napkins close by. Supply enough serving forks and spoons, and be sure they are appropriate—you know, don't put the pierced spoon next to the sauce.

You will find 48 party menus in this book. There are big parties and little parties, cocktail parties and buffets, elegant, informal and alfresco parties; and each party is planned down to the last radish.

In Chapter Nine you will find the calorie-reduced basics you use throughout. There, you will find a mayonnaise-type dressing (16 calories per tablespoon) to substitute for the real thing (100 calories per tablespoon); plus eight other salad dressings, calorie-reduced sauces, fat-free bouillons, a delicious crumb coating for chicken, chops or fish—all of which save you literally hundreds of calories per serving.

The Appendix lists brand names of certain calorie-reduced items I have found useful and that can be found without too much trouble country-wide.

As you see, I have given you all the ammunition you need to fight the ever-present battle of the bulge, so go forth and give a lot of really great low-calorie parties.

All in all, the hostess who entertains in this new, thoughtful manner, secretly reducing calories while still producing delightfully different, enticing food, will be loved by all her friends. As my friend Leon says, "We love to come to Suzy's—we know we won't get fat, but we'll get enough to eat." Follow my directions and a whole new world of parties will open up for you and your fortunate guests.

CHAPTER ONE

Cocktail Parties

*T*he cocktail party, be it large or small, is the answer to many social dilemmas. This is such a pleasant way of gathering friends together without the attendant problems of dinner tables, seating plans and other elaborate exertions. Everyone collects some social debts that sooner or later must be paid. Perhaps your house or apartment isn't large enough to have a sit-down dinner. Have a few friends in for a drink before another kind of party, such as a dinner dance. This can really get the evening off to a good start. If you are going to a sports event, it is fun to ask a few couples back to your place for drinks and nibbles.

Cocktail parties can be as simple as having one or two people over for a drink before dinner, or as grand as a splendid splash for thirty or more. It is really nice to relax at the end of the day with a convivial group.

Usually the first question I am asked is how is it possible to have—or go to—parties, and keep from gaining unwanted pounds. The average American cocktail party *is* woe to the waistline. There are ways to get around this problem, and this book is, in part, my attempt to make parties more fun and less fattening.

There are cocktail parties and then there are cocktail buffets (the next chapter contains menus for the latter). I like to send out "wordy" invitations that include definite time limits to the party: "Cocktails from Five to Seven," "Drinks from Six to Eight," "Before the Dinner Dance, Seven to Nine," whichever time is most appropriate. I try to identify the party "After the Game for Cocktails," "Open House: Cocktail Buffet, from Eight On." We have gone to many parties thinking they were simple "Come for Cocktails" and discovered the hostess placing a beautiful buffet on the table as we

Casual Cocktails for Twelve (page 12) provides
plenty of wholesome, appetizing nibble food to go
with drinks—yet menu keeps waistlines intact.

7

were taking our leave at seven-thirty. This is unfair to organized guests, and also disappointing to the hostess.

Numbers are important when planning a party, as well as the time. Do not invite too many guests—they might all come. You can probably handle up to twenty people without help. If you cannot find or afford professional help, enlist the aid of older teen-agers, or ask a close friend to assist in making drinks, cleaning up ashtrays and glasses, and passing hors d'oeuvres. If you plan to serve hot hors d'oeuvres there should be someone in the kitchen to keep them from burning. If you are having thirty or more guests it is wise to set up two separate bars.

Be sure to have enough ice. My husband says you can almost always borrow enough liquor to see you through if you should run out, but ice is often hard come by. If you don't have a freezer, bags of commercial ice will keep in styrofoam picnic boxes, which are inexpensive to buy. If you have a freezer, make extra cubes early in the week, place them in plastic bags and keep in the freezer. Make twice as much ice as you think you will need. That should be enough.

Have enough ashtrays, and a silent butler for getting rid of the ashes. I keep a large supply of big square ashtrays from the variety store. If you don't furnish plenty of ashtrays you will find ashes and stubs in the oddest places. Some of your furniture or rugs might be burned.

Use cocktail napkins. I prefer paper napkins because linen ones have to be ironed. Paper coasters are most practical. (Glass coasters get used as ashtrays and sometimes stick to the bottom of the glasses.)

The size of your pocketbook determines the size of your party. Unfortunately, the best food, dietetically speaking, can be quite expensive, like caviar, crabmeat, shrimp, lobster, and beef tenderloin. However, since these are a big success at any buffet table because they are low in calories as well as delicious, you should consider splurging. The largest item on your list is, of course, liquor. Consult your budget, make your guest list, and plan your party menu, both food and drink. Then make your marketing list. Pin the menu up in the kitchen so you won't forget something divine that you have placed in the refrigerator. Check the list as you serve.

I would never suggest serving drinks that are reduced in alcoholic content, such as making a Vodka and Tonic with half an ounce of vodka. Anyone who wants a small drink will say so—in fact, more and more guests today ask for a "light drink." I am assuming that you already know how to mix plenty of "real" drinks. For these it is very handy to have a supply of those little packets that enable you to mix a very professional whiskey sour, Tom Collins, margarita or other fancy cocktail. Low-calorie soft drinks and mixers are available in every supermarket, in a wide range of flavors, and you should have plenty of them.

Usually someone who is really dieting and sticking to it likes to have a drink in his hand at a party, even if the drink doesn't contain caloric liquor. People don't have to know everything.

So here I am giving you recipes mostly for nonalcoholic drinks that taste good and look like the real thing. Also included are three wine drinks that are relatively light in alcoholic content. My own favorite summer drink is sangria.

Bloody Shame

This is a bloody Mary without the alcoholic calories.

5 ounces tomato juice
Juice of ½ lemon
1 teaspoon Worcestershire Sauce
2 dashes Angostura bitters
3 to 5 drops Tabasco
Sprinkle of celery salt
Pinch of sugar (optional; it seems to smooth the drink, costs about 3 calories)

Stir all ingredients in a bar glass or pitcher with ice cubes, strain into an old-fashioned glass or footed 6-ounce tumbler. Or serve it on the rocks, by pouring over ice cubes already in the glass.

Serves 1.

Horse's Neck

8 ounces low-calorie ginger ale
Long spiral lemon peel

In a tall, slim highball glass pour ginger ale over ice cubes. Spiral a long piece of lemon peel, cut about ½ inch wide, down the inside of the glass.

Serves 1.

Seadog

3 ounces tomato juice
3 ounces clam juice
Juice of ½ lemon

Stir tomato and clam juices in a bar glass or pitcher. Serve in a highball glass on the rocks or straight up. A good squeeze of lemon juice on top sparks up this drink and keeps the scurvy away on the long voyage home.

Serves 1.

Sitting Bull Shot

This won't knock you over.

4 ounces canned beef bouillon
1 piece lemon peel

Pour undiluted canned beef bouillon over ice cubes in an old-fashioned glass. Squeeze the lemon peel over the top, skin side down, and drop the peel in the glass.

Or, if the night is cold and wintry, serve the bouillon steaming hot in a little mug.

Serves 1.

Apple Juice on the Rocks

This looks very much like Scotch, if you are interested in fooling the public. The taste is different, though.

4 to 8 ounces apple juice (*not* cider)

Pour apple juice over ice cubes in an old-fashioned glass for a short drink, or in a tall glass for a long one.

Serves 1.

Faded Madras

A real Madras has vodka in it, which raises the calorie count.

3 ounces unsweetened orange juice
3 ounces low-calorie cranberry juice

Place 3 or 4 ice cubes in a highball glass. Pour in the orange juice and the cranberry juice. Stir well.

Serves 1.

Cool as a Cucumber

This could probably pass for Pimm's Cup.

8 ounces unsweetened grapefruit
   juice
1 long spear of cucumber with rind
   on

Pour unsweetened grapefruit juice over ice cubes in a highball glass. Cut a cucumber into long spears (eighths is a good size) and stick a cucumber spear down the inside of the glass.

Serves 1.

Spritzer

A delicious drink that lasts a long time.

2 ounces dry white wine (Chablis, Soave, Pouilly-Fuissé, etc.)
Sparkling water

Pour wine into highball glass filled with ice cubes. Top off with sparkling water.
Serves 1.
Variation:
Substitute rosé wine for the white wine for a more festive-looking drink.

Claret Lemonade

Do not be tempted to use frozen lemonade for this drink, as it is full of sugar.

Juice of ½ lemon
Dash of liquid artificial sweetener
2 ounces claret
½ lemon slice
½ orange slice

Fill a tall highball glass with ice cubes, add lemon juice and sweetener, and fill glass to 2 inches from top with ice water. Stir well. Add claret and stir again. Garnish with lemon and orange slices.
Serves 1.

Sangria

This is a Spanish drink, made in a pitcher, for a group. There is nothing more refreshing on a sultry evening when you are sitting around on the patio waiting for a cool breeze.

1 bottle (a fifth) any dry red wine (Chianti, Bardolino, Mountain Red, Pinot Noir, etc.)
2 cups sliced fruit (oranges, lemons, fresh peaches, apricots, strawberries, etc., in any combination)
4 ounces lemon juice
4 ounces orange juice
2 7-ounce bottles club soda
8 or 10 ice cubes

Use the above amounts for a 3-quart pitcher. Put red wine (Spanish, American, Italian, Chilean, or whatever you happen to have) in the pitcher. Add the sliced fruits. Allow the fruits and wine to sit at room temperature for several hours if you wish.

At serving time add the chilled fruit juices, club soda, and ice cubes. Stir with a long-handled spoon and pour into stemmed glasses.

Serves 4 to 6.

Variation:

If you prefer to make this drink with white wine, use only peach and pear slices in place of other fruits.

Casual Cocktails for Twelve

Vegetables with Creamy Curry Dip
Liver Pâté en Gelée
Champignons Farcie
Miniature Swedish Meatballs
Halibut Teriyaki
Turnips Pickled Pink

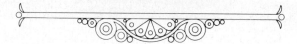

This is an international menu. You could use a cluster of paper foreign flags for a centerpiece. Each recipe has a different national origin, but most of them have been given an American accent. The meatballs can be served from a chafing dish, and the guests would enjoy cooking the Halibut Teriyaki on a Japanese hibachi.

Vegetables with Creamy Curry Dip

It is possible to buy calorie-reduced sour cream and cottage cheese. Take advantage of these calorie-saving items. The vegetables may be prepared the day before and kept in plastic bags in the refrigerator until serving time.

2 8-ounce cartons plain yogurt
1 cup calorie-reduced sour cream
3 tablespoons curry powder
Salt and white pepper to taste

1 bunch celery, cut in sticks
1 bunch carrots, cut in sticks
3 green peppers, cut in strips
3 cucumbers, peeled, seeded

and cut in sticks
1 fine medium cauliflower cut in flowerets
1 bunch radishes, cut in roses
1 bunch scallions, green tops trimmed

Mix the first 4 ingredients together. Place in a bowl and surround with a circle of the crisp raw vegetables.

Serves 12.

Liver Pâté en Gelée

These are elegant, delicious morsels that cost but 30 calories each.

4¾-ounce can liver pâté or 5 ounces soft liverwurst
1½ tablespoons calorie-reduced sour cream
Dash Tabasco
1 tablespoon onion, minced
1 envelope unflavored gelatin
¼ cup cold water
13-ounce can consommé madrilène
1½ tablespoons cocktail sherry
24 parsley sprigs
24 tiny cocktail onions
24 Melba toast rounds

Mix together liver pâté, sour cream, Tabasco and minced onion. Sprinkle gelatin over the surface of ¼ cup of cold water and let it soak for about 3 minutes until it has absorbed the moisture and is translucent.

Put consommé into a saucepan, add sherry, and bring to boiling point. Combine the soaked gelatin with the consommé and stir well until gelatin is completely dissolved.

Into each of 24 sections of a round-bottomed plastic egg tray (I use the one from my refrigerator), or round ice-cube tray, or tiny 1½-inch tart tins, put a parsley sprig, a cocktail onion, and ½ teaspoonful of the pâté mixture. Then fill carefully with the gelatin mixture. Refrigerate several hours, or until firm.

Have Melba rounds ready. To unmold: wring a clean dishtowel out in very hot water and place your egg-tray mold on this. The heat of the towel will soften the gelatin just a little. With a small, thin knife flip the gelatin out and onto the Melba rounds, flat side down. (Don't do this more than 1 hour ahead or the Melba toast will get soggy.)

Serves 12.

Champignons Farcie

These can be made ahead of time except for cooking. Either the day before or the morning of the party, stuff mushrooms as directed, place on cookie sheet, cover with plastic wrap, and refrigerate until cooking time. Remove plastic wrap before placing in preheated oven.

30 bite-size mushrooms (about 1
    pound)
1   tablespoon butter
2   tablespoons onion, minced
1   garlic clove, pressed
2   tablespoons green pepper, finely
    minced
2   tablespoons parsley, finely
    minced
½ cup seasoned bread crumbs
1   tablespoon wine vinegar
Salt and freshly ground black pep-
    per to taste

Remove stems from mushrooms,
reserving caps, and chop stems fine.

Melt butter in Teflon pan and add onion, garlic, green pepper, and parsley. Sauté over moderate heat until onion is limp. Add mushroom stems and continue cooking until juice appears. Mix in crumbs and vinegar. Season to taste with salt and pepper.

Stuff mushroom caps with this mixture. Place on baking sheet and put into preheated 350° oven for 15 minutes, just until bubbling hot. These can be kept warm on an electric hot tray.

Serves 12.

Miniature Swedish Meatballs

These melt-in-the-mouth meatballs can be made ahead of time and kept warm in a double boiler until you transfer them to a chafing dish.

¾   cup packaged herb-flavored
    bread stuffing
½   cup skim milk
2   pounds lean, ground round steak
½   cup onion, chopped
1   egg, beaten
½   cup parsley, finely chopped
1   teaspoon dried basil
1   teaspoon oregano
1   teaspoon nutmeg
Salt and pepper to taste
1½ tablespoons butter
1   tablespoon olive oil
½   cup calorie-reduced sour cream

Combine bread crumbs and milk and mix thoroughly. Add the ground

steak, onion, beaten egg, parsley, basil, oregano, nutmeg, salt and pepper. Mix until well blended. Form into tiny meatballs, using 1 teaspoonful for each one. (They are easier to roll if you dip your hands in cold water occasionally.) Place on cookie sheet, cover with plastic wrap, and chill for an hour.

Put butter and oil in a Teflon skillet and slowly brown meatballs on all sides. Do meatballs in several batches (depending on size of pan) until all are brown. As they are done, transfer meatballs to a double boiler or directly to a chafing dish and keep warm over low heat.

Add sour cream to the Teflon

skillet and mix well with the meat juices, scraping with a rubber spatula to get up all the brown particles. Reheat over low heat until just hot; do not allow to boil. Pour over meatballs. Serve from chafing dish, with toothpicks at the side.

Makes about 36, to serve 12.

Halibut Teriyaki

2 pounds halibut steak, fresh or
   frozen, cut into ¾-inch cubes
½ cup soy sauce
½ cup sherry
¼ teaspoon ground ginger
2 tablespoons honey or calorie-
   reduced maple syrup

Cut halibut into ¾-inch cubes. Combine remaining ingredients in a bowl (not metal), add halibut, cover with plastic wrap and marinate in refrigerator for several hours.

At party time, or shortly before, drain fish cubes and pat dry with paper towels. Skewer each cube on a presoaked bamboo skewer or metal skewer (page 34). Arrange skewers in rows on a pretty tray, cover with plastic wrap, and hold in refrigerator until ready to serve. Place tray beside a glowing hibachi and let your guests cook their own.

The fish can also be broiled in the kitchen, about 3 inches from heat, turning once, for about 2 minutes per side.

Makes 24 to 30 pieces, to serve 12.

Turnips Pickled Pink

A Lebanese lady gave me this recipe.

4 cups water
4 teaspoons salt
2 cups vinegar
2 pounds, small white turnips,
   peeled and cut in julienne strips,
   ½ inch by 2 inches
2 raw beets, peeled and sliced
2 garlic cloves, peeled

Heat water, salt, and vinegar just long enough to dissolve salt. Put turnips and beets in a bowl (not metal) and pour the pickling liquid over them. Add garlic cloves. Cover tightly with plastic wrap and let stand in refrigerator 24 to 36 hours. Drain turnips (discarding beets and liquid) and serve heaped on a pretty dish. (Guests can pick these up with their fingers.)

Serves 12.

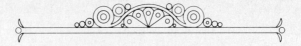

Elegant Cocktails for Twenty

Shrimp Bowl with Marjorie's Sauce
and Red Cocktail Sauce
Mushrooms with Scrambled Eggs
Pineapple-ham Kabobs
Dilled Carrots
Beef Balls Tartare

Twenty is a nice number to entertain when you have a special guest, a visiting relative, a college friend or an old neighbor back in town. There are enough people for variety and conversation so everybody can have fun.

Shrimp Bowl with Marjorie's Sauce
and Red Cocktail Sauce

Shrimp can be purchased all over the country at any time of year. Five pounds of shrimp should be enough, unless you invite some truly dedicated shrimp eaters. Not long ago I went to a party at which the hostess had made a large ring mold of ice, thickly embedded with seashells. It was stunning, and so easy to do. She placed the ring mold on a silver tray on a wheeled table and filled the ring with shrimp; the table was shoved from spot to spot on the terrace. There were two kinds of sauces, one based on mayonnaise, the other red. It was a hot evening and melting ice had to be siphoned off occasionally. Marjorie's Sauce keeps very well in the refrigerator, covered, so if you have some left over you can use it again a week or two later.

5 pounds shrimp, fresh or frozen, cooked, shelled and deveined
Ice bowl

Marjorie's Sauce
2 recipes Calorie-reduced Mayonnaise (page 187)
1 cup bottled steak sauce

¼ cup prepared mustard
1 tablespoon dark brown sugar
6 drops Tabasco
½ cup Parmesan cheese, freshly grated

Mix all ingredients together and chill until serving time.

Red Cocktail Sauce

3 7-ounce bottles cocktail sauce
3 tablespoons prepared white horse-
    radish
3 drops Tabasco

Mix all ingredients together and chill until serving time.

To assemble and serve: unmold ice bowl (directions for unmolding on page 117) onto silver tray with rim deep enough to catch melting ice water. Place chilled shrimp in center and place sauces in separate bowls on each side. Serve with toothpicks.

Serves 20.

Mushrooms with Scrambled Eggs

40 large mushrooms
2 cups Fat-free Chicken Bouillon
    (page 192 or 193)
12 eggs
4 tablespoons parsley, chopped
1 teaspoon dried basil
1 teaspoon salt
Freshly ground black pepper
2 tablespoons skim milk
1 pimiento, for garnish
Parsley sprigs, for garnish

Gently wipe mushrooms clean. Snap off stems, chop fine and reserve. Heat chicken bouillon in a skillet, add mushroom caps and poach gently, covered, 10 minutes. Drain mushrooms, set aside and keep warm. (Save broth for mushroom soup at some later time.)

Mix eggs with chopped parsley, basil, salt, pepper, skim milk, and the reserved chopped mushroom stems. Turn egg mixture into a Teflon skillet and scramble over moderate heat, using no fat, stirring constantly. As soon as eggs are creamy looking (in just a few minutes), remove from fire and spoon into mushroom caps.

Place on a heated serving dish; garnish each with a speck of pimiento and a parsley sprig. Keep warm on an electric hot tray or over a candle flame.

Serves 20.

Pineapple-ham Kabobs

2 20-ounce cans of pineapple
    chunks, packed without sugar
3-pound canned boneless ham, cut
    in 1-inch cubes
3 large green peppers, cut in 1-inch
    squares
½ cup soy sauce
¼ cup sake or dry white wine
¼ cup orange juice

Place alternate pieces of pineapple, ham and green pepper on skewers. (You may use leftover baked ham if you have it.) Combine soy sauce, sake, and orange juice in a shallow dish. Place the kabobs in it, keeping handles dry on the rim. Let marinate for at least 1 hour, even overnight in refrigerator.

Drain the marinated kabobs and place on a tray next to a glowing hibachi on one end of the buffet table. Your guests can do their own cooking. The kabobs can also be broiled in an oven: broil 3 inches from heat, turning once, for 6 minutes or more, until pineapple is turning brown on edges.
Serves 20.

Dilled Carrots

Dilled carrots are very low in calories, yet delicious. Inexpensive to make at home, they command a fancy price in the supermarket.

2   pounds carrots
¾ teaspoon cayenne pepper
3   stalks fresh dill (or 3 tablespoons dill weed)
3   cloves garlic, peeled
1   pint water
¼ cup salt
1   pint vinegar

Clean carrots and cut in uniform-size strips. Pack neatly in hot sterilized jars (3 1-pint jars should be enough). To each jar add ¼ teaspoon cayenne pepper, 1 stalk dill, 1 clove garlic. Heat together the water, salt and vinegar. Bring to a boil. Pour over vegetables in jars, filling to ½ inch from top. Seal at once.

Place jars on rack in a large kettle of boiling water. The water should cover jar tops by at least 1 inch. Boil 5 minutes, lid off, then set jars aside to cool. When jars are cool enough to handle, check to see that seal is tight. Store jars in cupboard for at least 2 weeks before using. Chill before serving.
Serves 20 to 25.

Variation:
Substitute 2 pounds small tender green beans for carrots. Wash and stem beans, leaving them whole. Pack neatly in sterilized jars, and follow directions above.

Beef Balls Tartare

1½ pounds lean ground round steak, ground twice
1   egg yolk
1   teaspoon salt
1   tablespoon Worcestershire Sauce
2   tablespoons grated onion
Freshly ground black pepper, to taste
2   tablespoons capers
Watercress

Radishes for garnish

Mix all ingredients except capers, watercress and radishes. Shape meat into 1-inch balls and put a caper in the center of each one. Keep tightly covered with plastic wrap in the refrigerator until serving time.
Place on a bed of crisp watercress, garnished with red radish roses.
Serves 20.

Cocktails on the Patio for Thirty

Brussels Sprouts with Caviar
Frannie's Curried Tuna Dip
Deviled Eggs
Turkey Amandine
Steak Teriyaki

When the weather warms up we all head for outdoors. The patio, screened porch, terrace or just plain back yard will do. Dust off the barbecue and ask the crowd to come share the sunset. Everything on the menu can be prepared before the guests arrive, leaving you to enjoy the party.

Brussels Sprouts with Caviar

Preparing the brussels sprouts takes time, but you can do it the night before the party while watching television.

3 pint boxes fresh brussels sprouts
3 3-ounce jars red caviar
Grated peel of 3 lemons

Blanch brussels sprouts by plunging them into boiling water for 3 minutes. Drain well and cool. Remove outer leaves and even off the bottom of each one so it will sit flat. Hollow out centers. Refrigerate until time to stuff.

Fill each center with a teaspoonful of caviar and sprinkle with grated lemon peel. Place on a serving dish, cover with plastic wrap, and return to refrigerator until serving time.

Serves 30.

Frannie's Curried Tuna Dip

2   teaspoons instant minced onion
1   tablespoon lemon juice
2   6½-ounce cans water-packed
    tuna
1   cup bottled calorie-reduced
    mayonnaise (see Appendix)
1½ teaspoons curry powder, or
    more, to taste
2   5-ounce cans water chestnuts,
    drained and minced
Salt and pepper to taste
2   bunches celery, cut into dipping
    sticks

1   package Melba toast rounds

Let onion stand in lemon juice 5 minutes. Combine with remaining ingredients except celery and Melba rounds, mix well, and place in a saucepan. Heat, but do not allow to boil, then transfer it to a small (1-quart) casserole over a candle. Have celery stalks nearby for dipping, as well as little Melba toast rounds.

Serves 30.

Deviled Eggs

3 dozen hard-cooked eggs
1 pint calorie-reduced sour cream
3 teaspoons anchovy paste
4 teaspoons celery seed
2 teaspoons Worcestershire sauce
2 teaspoons onion juice
Dash of Tabasco
6 drops garlic juice
Salt and pepper to taste
Paprika
Watercress or parsley garnish

Shell eggs and cut in half length-

wise. Remove yolks; mash, and set aside, reserving whites. Combine remaining ingredients except egg whites, paprika and watercress. Mix well, and combine with mashed egg yolks.

Stuff egg whites with this mixture and sprinkle with paprika. Refrigerate, lightly covered with plastic wrap, until serving time. Serve on a bed of watercress or parsley.

Serves 30.

Turkey Amandine

These are filling enough to satisfy the heartiest eater, high in protein and low in calories. The coating of almonds is so thin that the calorie count per piece is negligible. Use the cooked breast of a 15-pound turkey, or a frozen 2-pound package of white meat of roast turkey found at many supermarkets, which you cook according to directions on package.

1 breast of turkey, roasted
2 recipes Calorie-reduced Russian
    Dressing (page 188)
2 cups sliced almonds
1 bunch (about 1 pound) white
    seedless grapes for garnish

With a very sharp carving knife, cut the turkey meat in ¾-inch cubes —cutting lengthwise first, then across—to make about 80 cubes. Push a toothpick into each cube.

Pour Russian Dressing into a pie plate. Spread sliced almonds on a cookie sheet and toast in a preheated 350° oven 10 minutes, or until lightly brown. Put toasted almonds into a blender and chop at high speed for 1 minute. (Do not grind them.) Pour chopped almonds into another pie plate.

Dip turkey cubes first into Russian Dressing, next into the chopped toasted almonds.

Arrange the coated cubes on a silver platter and garnish with tiny clusters of white seedless grapes.

Serves 30.

Steak Teriyaki

You can buy bags of frozen, tiny white onions at the supermarket. It saves all that peeling and eye watering.

1 cup soy sauce
½ cup dry white wine
1 teaspoon ground ginger
2 garlic cloves, minced
2 tablespoons brown sugar
5 pounds sirloin steak or filet of
    beef
2 pint boxes cherry tomatoes
1-pound bag small white onions,
    frozen

Make a marinade by mixing together the first 5 ingredients. Cut well-aged steak or filet of beef into bite-size cubes, put into a bowl (not metal), and pour the marinade over them. Cover with plastic wrap and place in refrigerator overnight.

Wash cherry tomatoes. Plunge frozen onions into boiling water 3 minutes to soften them. Drain well and cool.

Lift the beef cubes out of the marinade, drain, and pat dry with paper towels. Thread on presoaked bamboo skewers or metal skewers (page 34), alternating pieces of beef with cherry tomatoes and onions. Arrange loaded skewers on trays, cover with plastic wrap, and hold in refrigerator until ready to serve.

At serving time, have twin hibachis at two different locations, already loaded and ready to cook (see hibachi instructions on page 34). Bring out the trays of teriyaki and let the guests do their own cooking.

Serves 30.

After the Game Cocktails for Sixteen

Deviled Clam Balls
Ham Pâté
Gherkin Fans
Cauliflower with Ruth's Dip
Pickled Melon
Miniature Lamb Kabobs

As the sound of cheering dies away, it is heart-warming to have a place to go, be it to celebrate the victory or mourn the loss. Set the table before the game, and have everything assembled ready to go as soon as you return to the house. Start the charcoal for the hibachi (see hibachi instructions on page 34) while the clam balls are broiling.

Deviled Clam Balls

1   large onion, finely chopped
1   large green pepper, finely chopped
2   cloves garlic, finely chopped
2   stalks celery, finely chopped
2   tablespoons olive oil
2   7-ounce cans minced clams with juice
1½ cups cracker crumbs
2   tablespoons Worcestershire sauce
Dash of Tabasco
1   tablespoon soy sauce
1   tablespoon prepared horseradish

Put chopped onion, green pepper, garlic, and celery into a Teflon pan and sauté in 1 tablespoon of the olive oil until soft.

Put clams and their juice into a bowl and add the sautéed onion mixture and the rest of the ingredients. Combine well and roll into 1-inch balls with your hands. Brush outside of each ball with remaining oil. Place on cookie sheet, cover with plastic wrap, and refrigerate until cooking time.

Broil, turning to brown on all sides, 3 inches from heat in preheated broiler, for about 6 minutes in all.

Makes about 60 1-inch balls, to serve 16.

Ham Pâté

This pâté can be made the day before and held in the refrigerator (covered with plastic wrap) until party time.

2 cups lean ham, cooked and cubed
½ cup evaporated skim milk
4 tablespoons tomato catsup
1 tablespoon Worcestershire sauce
1 cup celery, finely chopped
3 tablespoons onion, finely chopped
Dash of Tabasco
1 package rye Melba rounds

Place all ingredients except Melba rounds in the blender. Blend at high speed for 3 minutes, or until smooth. Mound in an attractive dish, and surround with rye Melba rounds. Don't forget to place a spreader nearby.

Serves 16.

Gherkin Fans

3 8-ounce bottles sweet gherkin pickles, about 2 inches long

Drain pickles, saving juice for pickled melon balls (page 24). Cut each pickle in thin slices almost to the end. Press with your fingertip to make them spread out so they resemble little fans.

Put on a dish, cover with plastic wrap and refrigerate until serving time.

Serves 16.

Cauliflower with Ruth's Dip

The sauce is pink, the cauliflower white, and together they make a pretty plate. You can add other raw vegetables if you wish, but cauliflower is so popular around this house I usually serve it alone.

2 recipes Calorie-reduced Mayonnaise (page 187)
1 cup tomato catsup
2 medium onions, finely chopped
2 tablespoons lemon juice
4 teaspoons curry powder, or more, to taste
2 teaspoons chili powder
1 large, fine cauliflower

Combine all ingredients except cauliflower in a bowl and mix well. Taste for seasoning and add more curry powder if you think necessary.

Break cauliflower into flowerets and arrange around a plate with the bowl of dip in the center.

Serves 16.

Pickled Melon

1 large honeydew melon
2 cantaloupes
Juice from 3 8-ounce bottles of sweet gherkin pickles (reserved from Gherkin Fans, page 23)
½ cup red wine vinegar

Cut melons into balls. Put into a bowl (not metal), and add gherkin juice and wine vinegar. Cover with plastic wrap and marinate overnight in the refrigerator.

In the morning, drain melon balls well and pat dry with paper towels. Cover with plastic wrap and keep chilled until serving time.

Serve in a pretty bowl with toothpicks at hand for guests to help themselves.

Serves 16.

Minature Lamb Kabobs

4 pounds lamb, from leg or shoulder
2 cups dry white wine
2 teaspoons red wine vinegar
2 large onions, thinly sliced
2 bay leaves, crumbled
2 teaspoons salt
2 pints cherry tomatoes

Twenty-four hours or more before serving, trim meat of fat and cut in ¾-inch cubes. Place in a deep bowl (not metal) and pour over it the wine, vinegar, onions, crumbled bay leaves and salt. Cover and put into refrigerator to marinate overnight. (Turn the meat in the marinade once or twice.)

The afternoon of the party, lift lamb cubes out of marinade. Use small flat-bladed skewers; on each one thread 3 lamb cubes alternating with tomatoes. Set loaded skewers on a tray, cover with plastic wrap, and refrigerate until time to cook.

At serving time, set the lamb kabobs out beside the lighted hibachi and let your guests broil their own. (Or broil in your kitchen oven, 3 inches below the flame, for about 3 minutes on each side, or until browned all over.)

Serves 16.

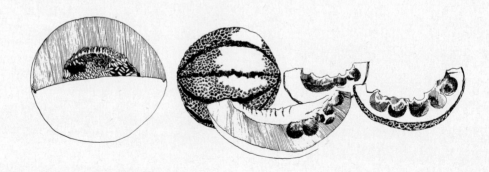

"Thank Goodness It's Friday" Cocktails for Eight

Cucumber-salmon Wheels
Snails in Mushroom Caps
Delicious Apples with Roquefort Dip
Beets Vinaigrette
Steak and Water Chestnuts en Brochette

Close friends and neighbors tend to gather and celebrate the end of a long week with a few relaxing drinks. Sometimes the party is continued as a Dutch Treat dinner at a nearby restaurant. Here's a cocktail menu to help start the weekend festivities, tiding you over till dinner without adding burdensome calories.

Cucumber-salmon Wheels

3 large cucumbers
¼ teaspoon salt
¼ teaspoon freshly ground black pepper
¼ cup white vinegar
1-pound can salmon
½ cup calorie-reduced cottage cheese
2 tablespoons calorie-reduced margarine
Salt and pepper to taste

Fresh parsley, finely chopped

Peel cucumbers with vegetable peeler, leaving a few narrow strips of green rind. Cut each cucumber in half crossways. Cut ends off squarely, and remove seeds from centers, using an apple corer, leaving a shell about ½ inch thick. Sprinkle cucumbers with salt, pepper and vinegar, and stand on end in a bowl to drain for about 2 hours. Remove, pat dry with paper towels.

Take salmon from can, drain, and remove skin and bones. Mash with a fork and add cottage cheese, margarine, and salt and pepper to taste. Pack the salmon mixture as tightly as possible into cucumbers.

Wrap each stuffed cucumber in plastic wrap and chill thoroughly. Just before serving, unwrap and cut in ½-inch slices. Arrange slices on a dish and sprinkle with minced parsley.

Makes 18 to 20 slices, to serve 8.

Snails in Mushroom Caps

Snails used to be very hard to find. Now almost every specialty shop and many supermarkets have snails, not only canned, but frozen. As the frozen snails are heavily laden with butter, I prefer the canned.

2 tablespoons parsley, finely minced
2 tablespoons scallions, finely minced
4 garlic cloves, pressed
4 tablespoons calorie-reduced margarine
24 medium-sized mushrooms (1-inch diameter)
4¼-ounce can snails (24 snails)
Salt and pepper to taste

Mix parsley, scallions and garlic with softened margarine. Fill each stemless mushroom cap with parsley mixture. Place a snail on each cap and top with another dab of the parsley mixture. Place on a cookie sheet and bake in a 400° preheated oven for 10 minutes.

Serve with cocktail spears or toothpicks. Keep any extras on an electric hot tray.

Serves 8.

Delicious Apples with Roquefort Dip

For some reason Delicious apples when sliced do not turn brown as fast as other varieties.

8-ounce container calorie-reduced cottage cheese
¼ cup calorie-reduced bottled blue cheese dressing
1 tablespoon Worcestershire sauce
3 tablespoons Roquefort cheese, or any blue cheese, crumbled
4 to 6 large Delicious apples

Put first four ingredients in blender. Blend at high speed for 2 minutes, or until smooth.

Serve dip in bowl surrounded by an overlapping circle of thin slices of Red and Golden Delicious apples.

Serves 8.

Beets Vinaigrette

These keep very well, so you can make them at any time and have them on hand.

¼ cup boiling water
½ teaspoon salt
Freshly ground black pepper
1 teaspoon paprika
1 teaspoon sugar (or equivalent sugar substitute)
2 tablespoons vinegar
4 tablespoons olive oil
1 teaspoon prepared mustard
1 tablespoon onion, finely minced
1-pound can tiny whole beets

Combine all ingredients except beets to make a marinade. Put drained beets in a bowl (not metal), pour over the marinade, and cover and place in refrigerator for a day or two. Drain before serving. If you are feeling very festive, slice a piece off the bottom of a fine green cabbage (so it sits without wobbling) and stick the beets all over the cabbage on toothpicks.

Serves 8.

Steak and Water Chestnuts en Brochette

2 pounds sirloin or tenderloin steak cut in 1-inch squares
¼ cup soy sauce
¼ cup water
1 ounce bourbon
¼ teaspoon dried ginger
2 5-ounce cans water chestnuts

Cut meat in 1-inch squares. Combine soy sauce, water, bourbon and ginger in a bowl (not metal). Marinate the meat in this mixture, covered, overnight in the refrigerator.

Two hours before serving, remove from refrigerator. Drain the meat and pat dry with paper towels. Cut drained water chestnuts in half horizontally. Use presoaked bamboo skewers or metal skewers (page 34) and thread 1 meat cube and 1 piece of water chestnut on each. Arrange loaded skewers on trays, cover with plastic wrap and keep out at room temperature until time to cook.

Let guests grill steak over a hibachi, or put in the kitchen broiler (3 inches below heat) for about 3 minutes, or until brown all over.

Serves 8.

Cocktails before the Show for Twenty-four

Unorthodox Chopped Chicken Livers
Prosciutto and Melon
Egg Dip with Endive Leaves
Smoked Salmon Rolls
Chicken Bombay
Ginger-minted Carrots
Barbecue Baby Franks

There is more food in this menu than for the usual cocktail party, because it's designed to feed people enough to hold them until after a concert, lecture, theater performance, ballet, opera or whatever form of amusement is offered. This high-protein, low-calorie fare is filling and at the same time delicious and easy to digest.

Unorthodox Chopped Chicken Livers

Each time you buy a chicken, save the liver. Put it in a little plastic bag and tuck in the freezer. Soon you will have saved enough chicken livers to make this delightful but slightly different recipe. Low-calorie margarine has been substituted for the traditional chicken fat.

½ cup low-calorie margarine
2 large onions, finely chopped (to make 1 cup)
4 stalks celery, finely chopped (to make 2 cups)
1 sweet green pepper, finely chopped (to make 1 cup)

2 pounds chicken livers
2 teaspoons salt
½ teaspoon freshly ground black pepper
½ teaspoon ground cloves
6 hard-cooked eggs
1 package low-calorie crackers or

little round matzos (10 calories each)

Melt margarine in a Teflon frying pan, add chopped onions, celery and green pepper, and sauté over moderate heat until soft and onion is transparent. Cut chicken livers (while still partly frozen—it's easier that way) into quarters and add to pan with vegetables. Season with salt, pepper and cloves. Continue sautéing until no trace of pink remains in livers.

Meanwhile, hard-boil eggs. Shell them and place in chopping bowl. Add chicken liver mixture and chop very fine, until it has texture of crumbs.

Press into a bowl, or shape into a mound with your hands. Unmold bowl onto serving plate and serve surrounded with crackers; butter knives make good spreaders for this. Serves 24.

Prosciutto and Melon

Prosciutto is cured Italian ham. If you can't find it, any good smoked ham, sliced paper-thin, can be substituted.

3 large honeydew melons
1 pound thinly sliced prosciutto, or other smoked ham
Parsley sprigs for garnish

Cut the honeydew melons in chunks about 1 inch in diameter. Wrap a small piece of ham around each piece of melon and secure with a toothpick. Serve on a pretty tray, garnished with parsley.
Serves 24.

Egg Dip with Endive Leaves

This is like an egg salad sandwich without the bread.

1 recipe Calorie-reduced Mayonnaise (page 187)
2 dozen hard-cooked eggs, peeled and chopped
4 unpeeled red Delicious apples, finely diced and sprinkled with lemon juice
4 stalks celery, chopped
1 large green pepper, finely chopped (to make 1 cup)
24 pitted black olives, chopped
2 large red onions, finely chopped
Salt and pepper to taste
8 heads Belgian endive

Combine all ingredients except endive in a bowl, mix and chill. To serve: surround with individual Belgian endive leaves. The leaves are sturdy enough to use as scoops.
Serves 24.

Smoked Salmon Rolls

3 8-ounce packages Neufchâtel or other calorie-reduced cream cheese
2 pounds Nova Scotia smoked salmon
Watercress sprigs (or parsley) for garnish

Have cheese at room temperature so it is easy to spread. Have the salmon sliced thin, but not so thin it will tear. If it seems oily to the touch, pat dry with paper towels. Cut salmon into rectangles about 2 inches by 3 inches. Spread each salmon rectangle with the softened cheese. Roll up and fasten with a toothpick.

Place on a plate garnished with watercress or parsley.

Serves 24.

Chicken Bombay

4-5 pound stewing chicken, cooked (to make 6 cups minced)
6   artichokes, cooked
3   cups calorie-reduced sour cream
2   tablespoons curry powder
Salt and pepper to taste
2   large fresh pineapples

The day before, boil a 4- to 5-pound stewing chicken (as directed on page 48). When cool, mince enough of the meat (white and dark mixed) to make 6 cups. Combine minced chicken, sour cream, curry, salt and pepper. Put into a bowl, cover and refrigerate.

Before cooking the artichokes, wash them under running water, cut the points off the leaves, and then level the bottoms so they will sit flat.

Place in a large kettle filled with boiling salted water. Boil, covered, about 45 minutes, or until tender when pierced with a small pointed knife. Set to drain on paper towels.

Cut pineapples in half lengthwise, right through the foliage at the top. (An electric knife is helpful for this.) Hollow out pineapple halves, leaving a ½-inch shell. (Save the pulp for tomorrow's dessert.) Mound the chicken mixture into the pineapple shells.

Place pineapples on a large platter and surround with artichokes. People can pull off the artichoke leaves and use them to pick up the Chicken Bombay.

Serves 24.

Ginger-minted Carrots

You can do these way ahead of time, even a week, and hold in the refrigerator.

4 10-ounce packages frozen baby
  carrots
1 cup orange juice
2 teaspoons grated fresh ginger (or
  1 teaspoon ground ginger)
Salt and pepper to taste
4 teaspoons chopped fresh mint

Combine frozen carrots, orange

juice, ginger, salt and pepper in a
saucepan. Cover and bring to a boil.
Simmer until carrots are crisply tender, about 3 minutes. Drain, put into
covered bowl and chill until needed.
    Place in serving dish, sprinkle
with mint, and serve with toothpicks.
    Serves 24.

Barbecue Baby Franks

1 recipe Barbecue Sauce (page 190)
4 pounds tiny cocktail frankfurters

Make Barbecue Sauce. At serving
time place sauce in a chafing dish,

or in a casserole over a candle. Add
frankfurters to bubbling sauce. Have
toothpicks and a dish of mustard
close by for dunking.
    Serves 24.

CHAPTER TWO

Cocktail Buffets

A cocktail buffet is a more elaborate occasion than a cocktail party. When people are invited to a cocktail buffet they expect to stay on into the evening and be served with substantial food. I usually divide a cocktail buffet, like Gaul, into three parts. One: hors d'oeuvres; two: meat, vegetable and salad; three: dessert and coffee.

Part one: the hors d'oeuvres are handled as for a cocktail party—pretty dishes and trays of food are handed around the living room as guests are having predinner drinks. Dishes can also be placed around the room on side tables or cocktail tables so people can help themselves. This keeps the dining room free for the main part of the meal.

Part two: the main courses are set out on the dining room table (along with stacks of plates, napkins, silver and condiments). Dishes are put out in order so guests progressing around the table can help themselves to meat, then to the vegetables and garnishes, and finally to the salads. If you have no dining room, set up a large table (in the foyer, if you can, even in the dinette—in any case, it should be at the side, away from the center of the party).

Part three: dessert and coffee should be placed on the dining room table after part two has been cleared away—this includes everything, guests' plates as well as serving dishes and glasses; and don't forget to empty the ashtrays and remove hors d'oeuvres dishes from the living room. Although dessert and coffee can be served in the dining room, I find that people are reluctant to come back in to pick up their sweet and coffee, so I prefer to pass them around. A coffee urn may be placed on the dining room table (or the buffet table, wherever it is) so that guests may help themselves to refills.

One amusing thing to do at a party is to let your guests cook little goodies on a charcoal hibachi. Getting the charcoal to the proper glow was always a problem for me, until one of my most gifted friends showed

*A colorful cocktail buffet with Russian motif
(page 58) features a calorie-reduced Beef Stroganoff
and other Slavic fare in low-calorie form.*

me what to do. Take enough charcoal briquettes to fill your hibachi, place them directly on the large burner of your stove (either gas or electric will do), turn the burner to high, and let charcoal get glowing hot. Transfer to your hibachi with tongs and you are in business. If you are able to find little bamboo skewers (many mail-order houses carry them), use them, and always soak them well in water before using. (This keeps them from burning.) Or use metal skewers, being sure they have flat or square blades— round ones merely make the food revolve crazily about, and you can't turn them satisfactorily.

A cocktail buffet is an easy place to introduce a variety of low-calorie food without skimping on the quantity or quality. Party food can be fun and delicious, the dishes you serve looking just as tempting as their fattening originals.

The up-to-date hostess is calorie-conscious. Stand quietly behind a line of people at a buffet. Listen to the phrases that drift back to you. "I'll forget my diet." "I know I shouldn't. . . ." "Delicious, but so fattening!" "How can I resist?" "I'll go back on my diet tomorrow." Music to my ears are the words of the man who says he loves to come to our house because he can dine well without overdoing.

Traditional Cocktail Buffet for Twenty-four

I
Hot Cheese and Crab Dip
Wendy's Party Pâté
Fresh Vegetable Platter

II
Roast Turkey
Baked Ham
Homemade Mustard Pickles
Spinach Ring with Baby Carrots

III
Bountiful Fruit Basket with Assorted Cheeses

This is an "any season" party. All the food is available the year round. It is for the times when a big party is indicated for holidays, celebrations, special guests and family gatherings, and they can be the happiest and least fattening events of the year. The foods in this menu are easy to prepare—a boon to the busy hostess. One turkey or one ham will not by itself serve 24 people. Both of them together will be ample for a buffet supper, with all the accompanying dishes.

Hot Cheese and Crab Dip

4 16-ounce containers calorie-reduced cottage cheese (to make 8 cups)
2 10-ounce sticks sharp Cheddar cheese, crumbled
1 cup Chablis (or other dry white wine)
4 7-ounce cans crabmeat, picked over, rinsed, drained, and shredded

Place cottage cheese, Cheddar cheese, and wine in blender, a quarter of the ingredients at a time.

Blend at high speed for 1 minute. After blending each portion, place in saucepan, stirring well after last addition.

Heat cheese mixture over low heat, stirring occasionally. Add the shredded crabmeat, reserving several larger pieces for garnish.

Place in a chafing dish over a low flame (or in a casserole over a candle warmer, or on an electric tray). Garnish with reserved crabmeat.

Serves 24.

Wendy's Party Pâté

This delectable pâté can be unmolded an hour or two before the party and held in the refrigerator, lightly covered with an aluminum foil tent.

½ 10½-ounce can beef consommé, slightly chilled
6 4¾-ounce cans liver pâté
4 4½-ounce jars chopped mushrooms
4 tablespoons brandy
½ cup calorie-reduced sour cream
Watercress, parsley, or chicory for garnish
2 boxes Melba toast rounds

The day before the party, place slightly chilled consommé, still slightly runny, in a very cold 4-cup mold (preferably Teflon-lined) or round bowl. If the consommé is too hard, let it remain at room temperature until it softens. Tilt the mold to coat all sides and pour off excess. Place mold in refrigerator to harden. Repeat this process at ½-hour intervals until ½-inch coating of jelled consommé has been built up. Return to the refrigerator.

Put the pâté, mushrooms, brandy and sour cream into the blender. (Do this in several batches so as not to overload the blender.) Blend at high speed 1 minute, until smooth. Spoon carefully into the chilled mold, cover with plastic wrap, and refrigerate overnight.

Unmold carefully on serving plate (as directed on page 117). Garnish with watercress, parsley, or chicory. Serve with small Melba toast rounds. Serves 24.

Fresh Vegetable Platter

This is the delight of the weight-conscious party goer. How many times have I been reduced to eating the radish roses used to garnish the hors d'oeuvres tray! Years ago there was a restaurant in New York that served raw vegetables embedded in tall mounds of cracked ice. If I owned an ice-cracking machine this is how I would serve what the French call "crudités." Since I don't, I use a big lazy Susan. Mine has six compartments arranged around a large bowl in the center.

1 pound carrots, cut in sticks
2 bunches radishes, cut in roses
1 bunch celery, cut in sticks
2 bunches scallions
4 sweet green peppers, cut in strips
3 cucumbers, peeled, cut in strips and seeded
2 fine cauliflowers, broken into flowerets
Coarse salt
Seasoned salt

The vegetables should be prepared the day before, wrapped in plastic wrap, and held in the refrigerator.

At serving time put the cauliflowerets in the middle bowl with the other vegetables surrounding them. Small bowls of coarse salt and seasoned salt can be placed beside the lazy Susan.

Serves 24.

Roast Turkey

Turkey is beautifully low in calories, the white meat slightly lower than the dark. If you are lucky enough to live in a part of our country where you can buy a smoked turkey, you are indeed blessed. Place your bird on your biggest platter and garnish with spiced crab apples and parsley. Have the carving knife razor-sharp, and ask your husband or a talented friend to carve the bird. If you should have any left over, remember that it freezes well, the bones make wonderful soup, and the best part of a turkey is the "midnight carcass." If smoked turkeys are unavailable, roast a regular turkey. For a buffet, the bird need not be stuffed.

16- to 20-pound turkey
2 onions, chopped
4 ribs celery, chopped
Pepper and salt
1 cup dry white wine

Thaw bird, if frozen. It will take 2 to 4 days in the refrigerator, so start in plenty of time. If you get caught short and the bird is tightly wrapped in plastic wrap, place it under cool, running water for 2 to 6 hours. When the bird is thawed, rinse inside and out with cold water. Pat dry with paper towels.

To roast in heavy-duty aluminum foil, season inside and out with salt and pepper. Place chopped vegetables in turkey cavity. Place bird breast side up in the center of wide heavy foil at least 12 inches longer than the bird. (If the foil isn't wide enough, fold 2 pieces of foil to-gether.) Bring one side of foil up over turkey, then bring up other side, lapping it over the first one. Fold tightly and close the ends. The package does not have to be air-tight.

Place a meat thermometer through the foil into the thickest part of the thigh, not touching the bone. Place turkey in a shallow pan without a rack. Roast in a preheated, very hot (450°) oven for 3½ hours.

Take out of oven, remove foil, put back and roast for about ¾ hour more, basting every 5 minutes with 1 cup dry white wine. When the meat thermometer registers 170° remove bird from oven. It should be a delectable brown. Put it on a serving platter and allow to cool at room temperature. Do not slice until bird is cool.

Serves 24.

Baked Ham

I use a precooked (or canned) ham for this—it needs only heating through in the oven, which is done at the same time as the glazing. If you prefer, you may cook a ham to the point where it is ready to glaze. Whatever ham you use, this glaze adds a great deal to the flavor and appearance.

As with turkey, leftovers can be a joy. The grand finale is pea or lentil soup, using the ham bone.

12- 15-pound ham, precooked or canned
¼ cup prepared mustard
Whole cloves
1 cup bourbon whiskey
1 cup dark brown sugar
¼ teaspoon ground cloves

Fat should be trimmed from ham, leaving the thinnest film. With a sharp, pointed knife, score in diamond shapes, rub the prepared mustard into the ham, and stud at the diamond points with whole cloves. Put ham into shallow baking pan.

Combine bourbon, sugar and ground cloves, stirring to dissolve sugar. Pour evenly over ham.

Put ham into preheated 350° oven. After first 5 minutes, baste with the glaze that has dropped off to the bottom of the pan, and keep basting every 5 minutes for an hour or more. The glaze will be beautifully built up, dark and shining. Remove from oven.

Ham can be served at room temperature. Keep the mustard pot handy on the serving table. Have a really sharp knife for cutting paper-thin slices.

Serves 24.

Homemade Mustard Pickles

3   medium cucumbers, peeled and chopped
2   medium onions, finely chopped
2   red sweet peppers, seeded and chopped
1   medium cauliflower, broken into small flowerets
2   cups tiny whole white onions
½   cup salt
1½ cups brown sugar
2   cups cider vinegar
2   tablespoons dry mustard
6   tablespoons flour
¾   teaspoon turmeric
1½ teaspoons celery salt

Prepare vegetables. Place in a bowl (not metal) in layers, salting each layer, until vegetables and salt are all in. Add cold water to cover, and let stand overnight. The next day, drain vegetables and rinse well with cold water. Drain again.

To make mustard sauce, combine sugar and vinegar in a large pot and heat to boiling. Mix remaining ingredients in a bowl and stir in just enough of the hot sugar and vinegar mixture to make a paste. Then stir the paste into the rest of the boiling sugar and vinegar.

Add the well-drained vegetables to the pot and simmer, uncovered, until vegetables are tender but still crisp—crisp is the word. (This may take anything from 15 to 30 minutes, so keep testing.)

Cool, then turn pickles and sauce into a 6-cup bowl and chill until serving time.

Makes about 3 pints, to serve 24.

Spinach Ring with Baby Carrots

In order to serve 24 people it is best to make this recipe in three 8-cup ring molds. And if you're buying ring molds (who has three the same size?), be sure to get Teflon-lined ones—it makes the unmolding a joy instead of a ticklish job. This is served as a hot vegetable, and should be put in the oven just before serving, during part one of your party. The whole thing can be mixed, except for the folding in of the egg whites, early in the day. The finished spinach ring has a light texture, more of a timbale than a soufflé, however.

One Spinach Ring
(make three)

3 10-ounce packages frozen chopped spinach (to make 4 cups, cooked)
16-ounce container calorie-reduced cottage cheese, drained
1 cup packaged herb-seasoned bread stuffing
1 cup skim milk, scalded
8 eggs
1 large onion, grated
1 teaspoon salt
½ teaspoon freshly ground black pepper
½ teaspoon ground nutmeg
2 1-pound cans tiny Belgian carrots

Cook spinach according to package directions. Drain *very* well—place spinach in a double layer of cheesecloth and squeeze hard to remove remaining water. Put cottage cheese in a sieve and let it drain while the spinach is cooking.

Soak herb-seasoned stuffing in scalded milk. Beat together 4 whole eggs and 4 egg yolks. (Reserve the remaining 4 egg whites.) Add to the bread crumbs and milk. Add grated onion, salt and pepper. Mix drained spinach, cottage cheese and nutmeg with the herb-stuffing-milk-egg mixture. Beat the reserved egg whites until very stiff. Gently fold them into the spinach mixture.

Turn into a lightly oiled Teflon 8-cup ring mold. When you have filled 3 molds, place them each on a rack in a large pan of hot water, which reaches to the level of the spinach mixture. Bake in a preheated 325° oven 45 minutes.

At serving time, have 3 round platters ready. Run a sharp pointed knife around the inner and outer edges of the mold. Place serving dish on top of mold and, holding tightly to both, flip them over. The mold should lift off with no trouble.

Heat carrots in their own juice and drain well. Fill center of each ring mold with the warm, drained carrots and serve at once.

Serves 24.

Bountiful Fruit Basket

I usually make the fruit basket my table decoration in lieu of flowers. I have a large wicker horn of plenty, sprayed antique gold. From this base pour apples, pears, tangerines, grapes—in fact, any fruit, depending on the season. A pretty basket or large platter will do just as well. Fruit is best at room temperature. If you prefer cold fruit, chill and set out on bowls of cracked ice.

Peaches, plums and cherries are delicious additions during the summer. The greater variety of fruits you can offer the better. Melon shells can hold small fruits of the season such as strawberries, raspberries, blackberries and blueberries. Grapes drape so delightfully, and they taste so good.

6 red apples
6 golden apples
6 pears
3 tangerines
2 pounds seedless green grapes
2 pounds black or red grapes

Set out dessert plates with sharp knives and let guests help themselves to any combination of cheese and fruit that appeals to them.
Serves 24.

Assorted Cheeses

I have omitted crackers with the cheese board because we are serving a Bountiful Fruit Basket with it instead. Here are listed six different cheeses. A rough rule of thumb is a pound of cheese for each eight people, although it's hard to predict how much of one cheese will be eaten and how much of another will remain untouched. These cheeses contain from 85 to 110 calories per ounce, and two or three ounces per person should be plenty—for waist watchers, anyway.

Provolone is a sharp Italian cheese that goes well with seedless white grapes. Camembert with apples or pears is an old standby. A piece of well-aged Cheddar and a slab of Swiss make a lovely combination on the cheese board; both go well with a Dutch Gouda whose bright red coat is a standout at any party. Any leftover cheese will keep well. A five-pound wheel of Cheddar that made its debut on Christmas Eve at our house was finished in March—good to the last scrap.

1 pound Provolone, solid piece
Camembert, 24 wedges (unwrapped) at room temperature
2 pounds Cheddar, well-aged, solid piece
2 pounds Swiss cheese, solid piece
1 pound Feta cheese, solid piece
1 large Gouda cheese, top removed

Place the cheeses on two large cheese boards with a knife or cheese slicer for each one. Guests serve themselves, choosing whichever combination of fruit and cheese appeals to them.
Serves 24.

Springtime Cocktail Buffet for Twenty

I

Shrimp in Beer with Mustard Sauce
Stuffed Cherry Tomatoes
Pickled Beets

II

Corned Beef Maggie and Jiggs
Parslied Potatoes
Artichoke Hearts

III

Pears Flambée
Irish Coffee

Spring means more to me than apple blossoms. What about those April nights when soft rains fall? Consider when the March wind doth blow. Time to have a party all bright and happy. This menu has Irish overtones, but it is basically American.

Shrimp in Beer with Mustard Sauce

The mustard sauce should be made earlier in the day and kept chilled until serving time. We used to cook shrimp with their shells on and let the one who ate the most peel the most. This is a messy operation for a crowd, however, so clean and peel the shrimp in the morning.

4 egg yolks
1 teaspoon dry mustard
½ cup cider vinegar
¼ cup skim milk
2 tablespoons Dijon-type prepared mustard
2 tablespoons lemon juice
2 tablespoons brown sugar

6 12-ounce cans light beer
6 pounds large shrimp, peeled and cleaned
4 garlic cloves, pressed
4 stalks celery, cut in 2-inch lengths
10 whole peppercorns
Parsley sprigs for garnish

Make the mustard sauce first. Place egg yolks and dry mustard in a double boiler over hot water. Add vinegar and beat briskly with a whisk. Cook, whisking constantly, until thick. Add skim milk, continuing to beat. Cook 5 minutes more.

Take off the fire, cool, then add the prepared mustard, lemon juice and brown sugar. Mix well. Turn into a bowl and use as dip for shrimp.

To cook the shrimp, put the beer in a large kettle and bring to a boil. Add the shrimp, garlic, celery, and peppercorns, and cook, covered, for 5 minutes. Drain well. Serve shrimp in a casserole kept warm over a candle or on an electric hot tray. Decorate with parsley sprigs. Have toothpicks handy for spearing the shrimp to dip into the spicy sauce.

Serves 20.

Stuffed Cherry Tomatoes

Hollow out the cherry tomatoes the night before. This is a long job, but I put everything I need on a tray and watch a talk show on television while I'm working.

3   1-pint boxes cherry tomatoes, hollowed out
4-ounce bottle capers
3¾-ounce tin of tiny smoked oysters
½   cup calorie-reduced cottage cheese
2   teaspoons chopped chives
Salt and pepper
Parsley sprigs for garnish

Turn the tomatoes upside down on paper towels to drain. There are 3 different fillings, so divide tomatoes into three batches. For the first batch, drain capers and stuff a couple in each tomato. For the second batch, drain the smoked oysters and pat dry on paper towels to absorb the oil. Place an oyster in each tomato. For the last batch, mix cottage cheese with chives and salt and pepper to taste, and stuff the remaining tomatoes with that.

Decorate each tomato with a tiny parsley sprig. Set out on a silver tray, cover with plastic wrap, and keep in refrigerator until serving time.

Serves 20.

Pickled Beets

This can be done days or even weeks ahead.

3 16-ounce cans small whole beets
1 cup cider vinegar
3 whole cloves

Drain beets. Put beet juice in saucepan, add vinegar and cloves, and bring to a boil. Add beets and simmer 5 minutes.

Cool in covered container in refrigerator until time to use.

At party time, drain beets and heap in a bowl with toothpicks on the side. Or serve them impaled on toothpicks stuck into a large leafy cabbage as a centerpiece.

Serves 20.

Corned Beef Maggie and Jiggs

You must have a conference with your butcher and have him order the large piece of corned beef for you in advance.

10- to 12-pound slab corned beef
4 garlic cloves, slivered
8 whole cloves
3 onions
1 teaspoon freshly ground black pepper
4 bay leaves
2 tablespoons butter
1 tablespoon prepared mustard
⅓ cup dark brown sugar
⅓ cup catsup
3 tablespoons vinegar
3 tablespoons water

Soak corned beef 20 minutes in cold water, drain and wipe dry. With a small pointed knife make 1-inch incisions all over the meat and insert slivers of garlic in each. Stick the cloves in the meat.

Place beef in a kettle or roasting pan, and cover with cold water. Add the onions, pepper and bay leaves. Put the lid on, bring to a boil, then lower heat and simmer slowly 4 to 5 hours, or until tender. Remove from water. Pat dry and place in shallow roasting pan.

To make the glaze, melt butter, add remaining ingredients and heat until sugar has melted and sauce has blended. Spoon over the meat. Bake in preheated 350° oven 30 minutes, basting every 5 minutes to build up successive layers of glaze.

Serve hot, cold, or at room temperature. Slice half a dozen slices on the carving board, then let guests slice their own.

Serves 20.

Parslied Potatoes

Four or five of these little spuds count less than 100 calories, plus giving you as many vitamins as an apple.

6 1-pound cans tiny whole potatoes
4-ounce container calorie-reduced
margarine
1 cup finely minced parsley

Drain and rinse potatoes well under cold running water. Pat dry with paper towels. Melt the margarine in a saucepan and add the parsley. Put in the potatoes and gently heat them, turning them over so each gets its share of the margarine and parsley.

Serve in a casserole over a candle warmer or on an electric hot tray.
Serves 20.

Artichoke Hearts

2 recipes Calorie-reduced Mayonnaise (page 187)
6 9-ounce packages frozen artichoke hearts

Make the Calorie-reduced Mayonnaise, put into a pretty bowl, cover with plastic wrap and hold in the refrigerator until serving time.

Cook the artichoke hearts as directed on the package. Drain well, cool and serve at room temperature.

Place hearts on a dish, surrounding the bowl of Calorie-reduced Mayonnaise set in the center. Have toothpicks nearby for spearing hearts.
Serves 20.

Pears Flambée

This is a flashy finish to a great meal!

20 ripe pears
½ cup butter, melted
½ cup superfine sugar
10 ounces Irish Mist liqueur
10 ounces gin

Peel the pears and core them from the bottom, leaving them whole and with the stems on. Use a Teflon skillet so pears won't stick. Melt butter, then set in as many pears as will fit upright. Baste with the melted butter and cook over medium heat, basting often, for 7-10 minutes until pears are just tender, but not soft.

Repeat in batches until all the pears are cooked. Place cooked pears upright in a deep ovenproof dish that can also be used for serving, and keep warm.

At serving time, sprinkle sugar over the pears. Combine Irish Mist and gin in a saucepan and heat until warm. Set a lighted match to the heated liqueur and as soon as it flames, pour over the pears, spooning it over and over them until the flames die.
Serves 20.

Irish Coffee

20 tablespoons coffee
20 cups water
20 jiggers Irish Whiskey
3 4½-ounce containers calorie-
      reduced nondairy whipped
      topping

Use 20 tablespoons coffee in your usual grind and 20 cups water to make strong coffee in your usual way.

To serve, pour coffee into Irish coffee glasses (or any stemmed 5- or 6-ounce glasses). Add 1 jigger Irish Whiskey to each glass of coffee and top with a tablespoon of nondairy whipped topping.

Serves 20.

Cocktail Buffet in the Garden for Twelve

I
Mussels Ravigote
Bologna Cornucopias
Carrot and Celery Sticks with Black Olives

II
Shrimp-stuffed Eggs
Jellied Chicken Madeira
Hawaiian Coleslaw
Sour Creamed Cucumbers

III
Fruit Bowls with Juniper Juice

Summertime beckons us outside. Set your buffet table on a tree-shaded terrace, in a secluded patio, at the bottom of your garden, anywhere outdoors. Enjoy the soft summer sunset with your guests as you dine on heavenly morsels, with no caloric regrets in the morning.

Mussels Ravigote

Since mussels are very inexpensive, this recipe comes under budget shellfish. Delectable, too. Start the night before.

4   pounds mussels
A handful of flour
2   cups dry white wine
4   shallots
2   large onions, quartered
4   parsley sprigs
Dash of Tabasco
1   bay leaf
1   teaspoon dried thyme
Pepper
2   cups broth reserved from
        mussels, or bottled clam juice
3   tablespoons shallots, chopped
1   2-ounce bottle capers, drained
2   tablespoons fresh tarragon,
        chopped (or 1 tablespoon
        dried)
4   tablespoons parsley, finely
        chopped
1   pint bottled calorie-reduced
        mayonnaise (see Appendix)
6   tablespoons Dijon mustard
¼   teaspoon Tabasco
¼   teaspoon freshly ground black
        pepper

Scrub the mussels very well under cold running water to remove all sand and grit. Place them in a bowl of very salty water (sea water if you are at the beach). Throw in a large handful of flour. (Mussels will gorge themselves on it overnight, and emerge for your dish all white and plump and luscious.) Place bowl in refrigerator overnight. In the morning drain the mussels. Discard any that are not tightly closed. Rinse thoroughly.

Place the mussels in a large kettle with the wine, whole shallots, onions, parsley, dash of Tabasco, bay leaf, thyme, and pepper. Cover and bring to a boil. Simmer 10 minutes,

until all the mussels have opened. Lift out mussels and set to cool in a big bowl. Discard any that have not opened.

Strain the broth through a cloth-lined sieve. (I use a piece of old sheet; cheesecloth is too coarse.) Reserve 2 cups mussel broth; discard the rest.

As soon as the mussels have cooled enough to handle, remove them from their shells, saving half a shell for each mussel. Place mussels in half shells, put on a serving dish, cover with plastic wrap, and put in refrigerator.

Make the sauce *Ravigote*. First, boil the reserved 2 cups of mussel broth, uncovered, at high heat until reduced to ½ cup. Set aside.

Put the chopped shallots, capers, tarragon and parsley in a bowl. Add the mayonnaise to the bowl and with a wire whisk beat in the hot mussel broth a little bit at a time. Add the mustard, one-quarter teaspoon Tabasco and pepper. Cool the sauce to room temperature before using. (Keep the sauce in the refrigerator if not used within an hour; take out an hour before serving to return to room temperature.)

At serving time, take the tray of chilled mussels out of the refrigerator and neatly cover each mussel with a teaspoonful of the sauce.

Serves 12.

Variation:
Clams may be used, fresh, or the canned "steamers" that come complete with shells. Five 24-ounce cans should be ample.

Bologna Cornucopias

8-ounce container calorie-reduced
    cottage cheese
4 tablespoons prepared horseradish
2 teaspoons salt
Pepper to taste
1 pound Lebanon bologna, thinly
    sliced
Fresh parsley sprigs for garnish
    (optional)
Radish for garnish (optional)

Combine the cottage cheese,
horseradish, salt and pepper. Spread each slice of bologna with the mixture and roll into cornucopia shapes. Stick a parsley sprig in the top of each one, if you like. If they won't stick shut (they should), fasten with toothpicks.

Arrange on a round platter, like a wagon wheel, piling more parsley in the center, topped with a radish rose.

Serves 12.

Carrot and Celery Sticks with Black Olives

One manufacturer of pitted ripe olives is kind enough to state on the label of the six-ounce drained-weight can that "the olives in this can contain approximately 4 calories each." There are approximately 68 olives in that size can.

1 pound of carrots
1 bunch of celery
2 6-ounce cans pitted black olives

Cut carrot and celery sticks 3 inches long and ½ inch thick. Stick a pitted black olive on the end of each little stick.

Place in footed sherbet glasses and use as centerpieces on the platters that hold the Shrimp-stuffed Eggs.

Serves 12.

Shrimp-stuffed Eggs

This seems like a lot of eggs, but men really devour them.

½ recipe Calorie-reduced Mayon-
    naise (page 187)
2 dozen hard-cooked eggs
1 tablespoon Dijon-type mustard
1 teaspoon salt
½ teaspoon freshly ground black
    pepper
1 4½-ounce can of small shrimp,
    drained
Parsley sprigs for garnish (optional)

Make Calorie-reduced Mayonnaise. Hard-boil the eggs.

Peel and cut eggs in half lengthwise. Scoop out yolks, reserving whites. Mash yolks and add all ingredients except shrimp and parsley.

Fill the egg whites with the mashed yolk mixture and place one shrimp and a parsley sprig on each.

Serves 12.

Jellied Chicken Madeira

This is prepared the day ahead.

5-pound stewing chicken (or 2
    fryers), cut up
4   cups water
1   onion, sliced
1   carrot, sliced
2   celery stalks, sliced
3   sprigs parsley
2   teaspoons salt
¼   teaspoon white pepper
1   teaspoon dried tarragon
2   envelopes unflavored gelatin
1   cup Madeira wine
1   cup cooked carrots, cut into
    rounds
2   scallions, parboiled
1   jar large pimiento-stuffed olives
Chicory (or watercress or shredded
    lettuce)

Place the chicken in a stewing kettle with water, onion, carrot, celery, parsley, salt, and white pepper. Bring to a boil, reduce heat, and simmer 15 minutes. Remove the scum that has risen to the top of the pot. Continue to simmer, covered, 2 hours or more, until chicken is tender. (Fryers will be tender in about an hour.) Remove chicken from kettle.

Strain liquid and return it to the kettle. Boil rapidly, uncovered, until broth is reduced to 3 cups. Add tarragon; simmer 5 minutes. Strain broth again and place in refrigerator to chill. When the fat has congealed on top, remove all of it.

Early in the morning of the party day, heat up the defatted chicken broth. Sprinkle gelatin over wine and let soak 5 minutes to soften. Add wine and gelatin to hot chicken broth, stirring to dissolve gelatin. Taste for seasoning. Chill the broth until it becomes syrupy (it should have the consistency of unbeaten egg white).

Remove skin and bones from chicken and cut in bite-size pieces.

Lightly oil a loaf pan (9 by 5 by 3 inches). Pour ¼-inch layer of gelatin mixture into bottom of pan. Place in refrigerator to set. When it is firm, place on it a flower design of cooked carrot rounds, with long pieces of green scallions (parboiled 1 minute) as stems and leaves. Cover with another layer of aspic and return to the refrigerator to set. When the second layer has hardened, fill the pan halfway up with pieces of chicken. Arrange 2 rows of drained stuffed olives the length of the pan. Cover olives with the remaining pieces of chicken. Pour over the rest of the aspic—it should be slightly congealed so the chicken won't float. Chill in the refrigerator until serving time.

Unmold (as instructed on page 117) onto a platter of chicory, watercress, or shredded lettuce.

Serves 12.

Hawaiian Coleslaw

1 recipe Sweet Coleslaw Dressing
     (page 188)
1 large or 2 small cabbages,
     shredded
2 carrots, shredded
1 sweet green pepper, shredded
20-ounce can pineapple chunks
     (packed without sugar),
     drained

Make Sweet Coleslaw Dressing. Combine the rest of the ingredients. Mix well with dressing and chill. Serve in a large crystal bowl.
     Serves 12.

Sour Creamed Cucumbers

8 cucumbers, peeled, seeded and
     cut crosswise into ¼-inch
     slices
2 tablespoons coarse salt
1 teaspoon white vinegar
6 hard-cooked eggs
2 teaspoons Dijon-type mustard
⅔ cup calorie-reduced sour cream
1 tablespoon white vinegar
½ teaspoon sugar
White pepper to taste
12 small cupped lettuce leaves
2 tablespoons dried dill weed (or 1
     tablespoon fresh dill, minced)

Early in the day (or the night before) put the cucumbers in a bowl (not metal) with the salt and 1 teaspoon white vinegar. Cover, and place in refrigerator until needed.

When you are ready to use them, place in a large tea towel and wring out all the moisture.
     Hard-cook the eggs; shell, and remove yolks. Cut egg whites in julienne strips. Mix whites with cucumbers.
     Press yolks through a sieve into a bowl. Slowly beat in the mustard, sour cream, 1 tablespoon white vinegar, sugar and pepper. Pour this dressing over the cucumbers. Mix well. Keep chilled in a covered bowl (not metal) until serving time.
     To serve, place 12 small cupped lettuce leaves on a platter and fill each with a mound of the dressed cucumbers. Sprinkle with dill.
     Serves 12.

Fruit Bowls with Juniper Juice

A tray of fruit bowls is a colorful addition to your buffet table. These can be done early in the day. The longer the flavors meld, the better this will taste. They make a smashing finale to your summertime party.

6 small cantaloupes
3 pints strawberries
1 pint blueberries
1 tablespoon sugar
½ cup gin
4 tablespoons lemon juice

Cut cantaloupes in half. If you have time you can decorate them with sawtooth edges or scallops. Remove seeds and the stringy centers.

Scoop out some of the pulp to make room for the other fruit.

Clean strawberries and blueberries, cutting strawberries in half. Mix them well with the sugar, gin, and lemon juice and spoon into melon cavities.

Hold in the refrigerator (covered with plastic wrap) until time to place on the buffet at dessert time.

Serves 12.

Harvest Home Cocktail Buffet for Twenty

I
Caviar on Toast
Crisp Vegetables with Coarse Salt

II
Hungarian Goulash
Mashed Yellow Turnips
Sweet and Sour Red Cabbage

III
Applesauce Froth

This hearty fare is just right for a harvest. Autumn is the time of homecomings, and gatherings of friends after the summer. The bounty of our wonderful country is never more evident than at harvest time.

Caviar on Toast

6 3-ounce jars red caviar
2 large onions, finely chopped
3 hard-boiled eggs, yolks and whites
    chopped separately
2 boxes white Melba toast rounds

Fill a round serving bowl (silver is best) with cracked ice and sink one of the jars of chilled caviar in the center. Keep in freezer until ready to serve. You can replace the little jar as it is needed. (Or, if you would rather, you may empty all the jars into a larger bowl, and set that bowl in the cracked ice.)

At party time, put the caviar out in its ice bowl with a small spreader. Place around it the chopped onions and eggs in separate small saucers, each with a little serving spoon (a demitasse spoon is the perfect size), along with a tray of white Melba rounds. Do not make the canapés up in advance as the Melba toast gets soggy.

Serves 20.

Crisp Vegetables with Coarse Salt

2 pounds raw broad beans (fava
    beans)
4 bunches radishes
1 pound white turnips
2 bunches fennel (or 1 bunch celery)
Coarse salt

Shell the beans. If some of the radishes are long and thin, make several horizontal cuts to ¼ inch from the bottom, pressing them out into little accordion shapes. Round radishes can be cut to make rose petals.

Peel and cut turnips into sticks 3 inches long and ½ inch thick. Cut fennel (or celery) into vertical slices through the heart. Place prepared vegetables in bowls of ice water, cover, and keep in the refrigerator until serving time.

To serve, drain crisped vegetables and arrange them on a lazy Susan with a mound of coarse salt in the center dish.

Serves 20.

Hungarian Goulash

To insure removing all fat from the goulash, prepare it the day before, refrigerate, and when cold skim all the fat from the top. Reheat in time to serve. Any kind of ragout or stew tastes better the second day, you know.

4   pounds yellow onions, coarsely
     chopped
⅓   cup shortening
4   pounds beef chuck, cubed, fat
     removed
1   tablespoon salt
2   8-ounce cans tomato paste
1½ pounds veal shoulder, cubed
1   pound pork shoulder, cubed, fat
     removed
3   cups dry white wine
1   tablespoon paprika
½   teaspoon black pepper
1   pint calorie-reduced sour cream

In a large, heavy skillet sauté the onions in the shortening until they are golden and soft. Add the beef and cook over medium heat until all the redness has disappeared. Add the salt and tomato paste, reduce the heat, and simmer 30 minutes more.

Add the veal, pork, wine, paprika and pepper and continue to simmer 1½ hours more. Test for tenderness, and if not tender enough, simmer another ½ hour.

At this point put the goulash in a covered (not metal) bowl and refrigerate.

An hour before serving, remove all the congealed fat from the top and put the goulash into an attractive 3-quart casserole you can bring to the table. Cover and put over low heat until very hot. Remove from heat and stir in the sour cream a little at a time. (Don't let it boil once the sour cream is in!) Serve over a candle warmer or on an electric hot tray.

Serves 20.

Mashed Yellow Turnips

Turnips are a delicious low-calorie substitute for potatoes. One cup of mashed turnips contains 40 calories, as opposed to 230 for mashed potatoes.

5 pounds yellow turnips, diced
1 tablespoon salt
Freshly ground black pepper

Wash, peel, and dice the turnips. Place in a large kettle of boiling water. Add salt; cover, and boil 15 or 20 minutes, until tender. Drain. Mash with a potato masher.

Freshly ground black pepper brings out the flavor, so place the pepper grinder next to the turnips' serving dish.

Serves 20.

Sweet and Sour Red Cabbage

If the weather is warm I serve this dish cold; in cold weather it tastes equally good hot.

4 tablespoons bacon fat
6 onions, sliced
3 red cabbages, finely shredded
6 large apples, peeled, cored and
     diced

1 8½-ounce jar calorie-reduced
     grape jelly
1 cup red wine vinegar
2 bay leaves
Salt and pepper

Melt bacon fat in a Teflon pan, add onions, and sauté until limp and golden. Place the sautéed onions in a large kettle and add the shredded cabbage and the apples. Stir in the grape jelly and vinegar. Add seasonings. Cover. Simmer, stirring occasionally, for an hour or more, until the cabbage is tender. (If it seems dry add a little water.)

Serve in a casserole over a candle warmer.

Serves 20.

Applesauce Froth

In Hungary this dessert is called "The Witches' Froth."

7 pounds apples, stemmed
12 egg whites
Juice of 2 lemons
1 cup sugar
Orange slices and grapes for garnish

Bake the apples until very soft, about 1 hour, in a 350° oven. When the apples have cooled enough to handle, remove the peel and core.

Put the apple pulp through a food mill or sieve, or blend in the blender at high speed for 30 seconds. Do this in several batches. Chill applesauce in bowl (not metal).

Whip the egg whites with the lemon juice and sugar until the whites are stiff and form peaks. Gently fold into the applesauce.

Serve in a crystal bowl. Garnish with orange slices and grapes.

Serves 20.

Hearthside Cocktail Buffet for Twelve

I

Curried Shrimp
Spicy Mushrooms
Jeddie's Pâté

II

Blanquette de Veau
Beets à l'Orange
Hot Green Bean Salad

III

Lemon-orange Delight

When snow and ice crunch underfoot, what better time to welcome friends to your glowing hearth? Even if you don't have a fireplace, little hibachis can glow on your buffet table as the guests cook the curried shrimp.

Curried Shrimp

If it embarrasses you to make the fish man count the shrimp (36 are needed for a buffet for 12 people), you'll just have to guess and order two pounds.

½   cup mango chutney
2   pounds medium shrimp (36)
Curry powder
1¼ pounds sliced bacon (about 25 slices), **cut in thirds**

Purée chutney in blender at high speed for 1 minute. Boil the shrimp for 2 minutes in salted water. Drain and, when cool enough to handle, peel, devein and cut each shrimp in half.

Roll each shrimp in curry powder, put a dab of chutney (about ¼ tea- spoon) on each, and wrap it in ⅓ slice of bacon. Secure with a tooth- pick.

Broil about 3 inches from the heat for about 3 minutes on each side. Serve at once.

Or, if you have little hibachis, skewer each shrimp on a presoaked bamboo skewer or small metal skewer (page 34). Arrange on a serving tray, cover with plastic wrap, and refrigerate until serving time. Guests can then cook their own.

Serves 12.

Spicy Mushrooms

Prepare this a day or two ahead of the party. This lets the flavors blend.

2   pounds fresh button mushrooms
2   sweet green peppers
1   large onion, finely chopped
¼ cup olive oil
3   garlic cloves, pressed
½ teaspoon dried thyme
2   bay leaves
1   tablespoon ground coriander
Juice of ½ lemon
⅓ cup dry white wine
½ teaspoon salt
3   drops Tabasco

Wipe mushrooms clean with paper towels. Be sure they are dry. Cut green peppers in ¼-inch rings, dis- carding seeds and white membrane. Chop onion.

Put the oil in a large Teflon skillet. Add peppers, onion, garlic, thyme, bay leaves, coriander, lemon juice, wine, salt and Tabasco. Bring to a boil. Add mushrooms, reduce heat and cook softly 10 minutes more.

Put the mushrooms and sauce in a serving casserole, cover, and chill in the refrigerator until ready to serve. Serve with toothpicks.

Serves 12.

Jeddie's Pâté

This excellent pâté tastes as if you had been slaving over it all day.

1   large onion, cut up
2   cloves garlic, peeled
4   eggs
½   cup flour
1   teaspoon ground ginger
1   teaspoon allspice
1½ teaspoons salt
1½ teaspoons white pepper
¼   pound butter, softened
1   cup calorie-reduced sour cream
2   pounds chicken livers, halved
2   loaves thin-sliced party pumpernickel

Put the onion, garlic, and eggs into blender. Blend at high speed for 1 minute. Add flour, spices, softened butter and sour cream. Blend 2 minutes. Add chicken livers and blend 2 minutes more.

Pour into 9 by 5 by 3-inch loaf pan and cover tightly with foil. Set in a pan of hot water, put in preheated 325° oven, and bake 3 hours.

Remove foil. Cover the pan loosely with waxed paper and refrigerate for at least 4 hours, or better, overnight. Serve with paper-thin slices of pumpernickel.

Serves 12.

Blanquette de Veau

The classic Blanquette de Veau is rich and fattening with the egg yolks and heavy cream used to thicken it. I have used only calorie-reduced sour cream, and the taste is rich and delicious. Just the calories have been omitted.

3   tablespoons butter
2   tablespoons oil
2   medium-size onions, finely chopped
6   pounds breast of veal, boned, cut in 2-inch cubes, all fat trimmed away
⅓   cup flour, plus 2 tablespoons
1   teaspoon salt
1½ teaspoons dried rosemary
1½ teaspoons dried thyme
1⅔ cup fat-free bouillon, beef or chicken (page 192 or 193)
1   celery root, minced
1   stalk celery, minced
1   parsnip, minced
24 small white onions, peeled
4   carrots, sliced lengthwise
1   cup calorie-reduced sour cream
Parsley, finely chopped

Melt butter in large Teflon skillet, then add oil. Add onions and sauté slowly. Meanwhile, shake the cubes of meat in a paper bag with ⅓ cup of the flour and salt, rosemary and thyme.

When the onions are soft and beginning to turn golden, add the meat to the pan and sauté gently to seal all sides. Do not let it brown.

In another pan, heat the bouillon, then add it to the onions and meat with the minced celery root, celery, and parsnip. Cover and simmer very gently, so that it barely bubbles, for 30 minutes.

Lay the white onions and carrot sticks carefully on top of the stew. Cover and continue to simmer the stew over low heat for 1 to 1½ hours more.

Remove the meat, onions and carrots to a serving platter and keep warm.

Put the sauce into a blender with the remaining 2 tablespoons of flour and whirl at high speed for 1 minute. Return the sauce to the pot and cook for a few minutes to thicken. (If it seems too thick, add a very little hot water.)

Return the meat and vegetables to the pot. You can stop at this point and set the stew aside for an hour or two. If you are cooking it the day before, put it into a large bowl (not metal), cover, and refrigerate.

When it is close to serving time, put stew over a low flame, covered, until very hot but not boiling. Take off the stove and gently stir in the sour cream a little at a time. Reheat, but do not allow to boil.

Serve it in its own casserole or a pretty rimmed platter and sprinkle with chopped parsley at the last minute.

Serves 12.

Beets à l'Orange

3 16-ounce cans tiny whole beets
2 teaspoons vinegar
2 tablespoons grated orange rind
Juice of 1 lime
1 cup orange juice
3 tablespoons cornstarch
½ teaspoon nutmeg
1 cup beet juice
Salt and pepper
Chopped chives (or parsley)

Drain the beets, reserving 1 cup of the juice.

In a saucepan large enough to hold the beets mix the vinegar, orange rind, lime juice, orange juice, cornstarch. Add nutmeg and the reserved cup of beet juice, salt and pepper, and simmer, stirring, until the sauce thickens enough to coat spoon and becomes transparent. Add beets and stir to coat them with sauce. Warm through over low heat.

At serving time, put into a serving bowl and sprinkle with chopped chives or parsley.

Serves 12.

Hot Green Bean Salad

I call this a salad because the sauce is virtually a salad dressing. Dee-licious!

3 pounds fresh green beans (or 5 10-ounce frozen packages, French-style)
½ cup salad oil
2 tablespoons vinegar
½ teaspoon salt
¼ teaspoon freshly ground black pepper
2 teaspoons fresh rosemary (or 1 teaspoon dried)
2 cloves garlic, peeled

Put green beans in boiling water to cover, and cook until tender but still crisp (see directions on page 69). Drain well.

While the beans are cooking, combine the rest of the ingredients to make the dressing.

Put drained hot beans into a rimmed serving dish. Remove garlic and pour dressing over hot beans. Stir well. Serve at once.

Serves 12.

Lemon-orange Delight

14½-ounce can evaporated skim milk
½   cup sugar
1   envelope (½ of 2¾-ounce package) orange-flavor low-calorie gelatin
1½ cups boiling water
Juice of 2 lemons
1   tablespoon grated lemon peel
25   thin vanilla wafers, finely crushed
¼   cup butter, melted

Chill can of evaporated skim milk overnight in the refrigerator. Mix sugar with orange gelatin and dissolve in boiling water. Chill until almost set. Stir in the lemon juice and grated peel.

Whip the evaporated milk in a large bowl until it looks like soft whipped cream. Add orange gelatin mixture and continue beating for 2 minutes.

Pour the cookie crumbs evenly in the bottom of a 13 by 9 by 2-inch pan or Pyrex dish, reserving about 1 tablespoon of crumbs. Add the melted butter and press crumbs and butter firmly into the bottom of pan. Pour in the whipped lemon-orange mixture. Sprinkle reserved crumbs on top. Place in refrigerator until ready to cut in 12 squares and serve.

Serves 12.

Cocktail Buffet à la Russe for Twelve

I
Smoked Salmon
Sardine Fingers
Mixed Pickles
Eggplant Caviar

II
Beef Stroganoff
Tomatoes Gratinée
Salade d'Épinards

III
Strawberries Karenina

Russia is so huge and her heritage so varied it is hard to choose a menu that is representative. I think it is fun to have a party with a theme. If I had a samovar I would use it to make tea to serve with this dinner. Many years ago I met an elderly Russian gentleman who described himself as an "indigent teacher of the saber." He also liked to dine well, and my interest in Russian food goes back to those long-ago days.

Smoked Salmon

One of the world's great delicacies, smoked salmon, the Nova Scotia kind, is available sliced to order in most delicatessens. It is also obtainable in cans, but you must be sure to pat the slices dry with paper towels to remove excess oil.

2 pounds smoked salmon, thinly sliced (12 slices)
Parsley sprigs (optional)
Freshly ground black pepper
6 lemons, quartered

Roll up each slice of smoked salmon and arrange the little rolls next to each other on a platter. (Garnish with tiny parsley sprigs if you like.) Have the pepper grinder close by, and a plate of lemon quarters to add to the zest.

The guests serve themselves with toothpicks.

Serves 12.

Sardine Fingers

Small brisling sardines are the kind to buy. They must be patted dry with paper towels to remove excess oil. Calorie-reduced margarine (easy to spread) in a light film over whole wheat or rye thin-sliced bread helps anchor the little fish to the base.

1 loaf thin-sliced whole wheat or rye bread
Calorie-reduced margarine
3 ¾-ounce cans brisling sardines
Parsley
2 lemons

Remove crusts from thin-sliced whole wheat or rye bread, spread with margarine, and cut each slice into 3 fingers. Carefully take the little sardines from tins, drain and pat dry with paper towels. Set them out on a pretty plate and decorate with parsley.

Guests serve themselves. They place one little sardine on each bread finger, and give each sardine a bath by squeezing a little fresh lemon juice on it.

Serves 12.

Mixed Pickles

Pickles go well with fish, and there are so many different kinds to choose from. Delight yourself with several dishes of various types: garlic dill, sweet little gherkins, mustard pickles and bread-and-butter pickles.

2 whole garlic dill pickles, from the
delicatessen
16-ounce jar midget sweet gherkins
16-ounce jar mustard pickles
16-ounce jar bread-and-butter
pickles

Slice the garlic dill pickles into
½-inch rounds. The others are served
whole.

Set them out in a number of small
dishes at various spots around the
table, with toothpicks handy for
spearing them.

Serves 12.

Eggplant Caviar

This is called caviar because of its faint resemblance to the real thing. It
should be made the day before.

2 large eggplants
4 tablespoons olive oil
6 small onions, finely chopped
2 sweet green peppers, finely
chopped
4 garlic cloves, pressed
4 large ripe tomatoes, peeled,
seeded, and chopped
1 teaspoon sugar
1 tablespoon salt
½ teaspoon freshly ground black
pepper
4 tablespoons lemon juice
8-ounce package rye chip crackers

Put the eggplants on a rack in a
baking pan. Place in a preheated 425°
oven and bake for about an hour,
turning once or twice, until they are
soft and the outside is charred and
blistered.

Meanwhile, heat 2 tablespoons of
the oil in a Teflon-lined pan, add
the chopped onions, and sauté gently
for about 5 minutes, until they are
soft and golden but not brown. Add
the green pepper and garlic and
sauté, stirring occasionally, for 5
minutes more. Scrape the contents
of the pan into a large bowl (not
metal).

Skin the baked eggplants and chop
the pulp until it is nearly puréed. Put
the chopped eggplant in the bowl
with the onion mixture and add the
tomatoes, sugar, salt and pepper.
Mix everything well.

Put the remaining 2 tablespoons
of oil in the Teflon pan and pour in
the contents of the bowl. Bring to a
boil, stirring constantly, then turn
heat to low, cover, and simmer for
an hour. Remove the cover and simmer 30 minutes more, stirring so it
will not stick. It will be done when
it is very thick, but still moist. Stir
in lemon juice and taste for seasoning. Put into a bowl (not metal),
cover, and chill.

Turn out into a pretty dish and
serve as a spread with rye chip
crackers.

Serves 12.

Beef Stroganoff

This Beef Stroganoff tastes good and rich, but will not show up on the scales the next morning as added weight. It is best to use beef tenderloin for this because other cuts do not cook tender in as short a time. (A Stroganoff made with chuck steak would take several hours to cook.) The dill pickle added at the end of the recipe is a touch suggested to me by the late Henri Soulé of Le Pavillon; it gives subtle flavor to a delicious dish.

3 pounds lean beef, preferably
    tenderloin
4 tablespoons oil
4 large onions, finely chopped
2 pounds fresh mushrooms, sliced
    through stem
2 tablespoons flour
2 cups Fat-free Beef Bouillon
    (page 192 or 193)
Salt and freshly ground black
    pepper, to taste
1 cup calorie-reduced sour cream
1 dill pickle, finely minced

The first step is to cut the meat into strips; the job is easier if the meat is partially frozen. Cut across the grain into 2-inch strips about ¼-inch thick.

Heat 2 tablespoons of the oil in a Teflon pan, add chopped onions and mushrooms, and cook gently for about 25 minutes. When the vegetables are soft, drain them, pressing out the liquid. (Mushrooms give off a lot of liquid.)

In another pan heat the remaining 2 tablespoons of oil and quickly brown the meat in it. Do it in batches, just enough to cover the pan—a minute on each side should be enough. As the meat browns, add it to the cooked vegetables in the other pan. When all the meat is browned, add flour to the meat pan. Add beef bouillon and stir over medium heat until it is thickened. Add salt and pepper to taste.

Take off the fire, and slowly add the sour cream, stirring constantly with a whisk. Pour sauce over the meat in the first pan, add the finely minced dill pickle, and put over a low fire until hot. (Do not let it boil after you have added the sour cream or the sauce will curdle.)

Serve in a chafing dish if you have one, or in a casserole over a candle warmer or on an electric hot tray.

Serves 12.

Tomatoes Gratinée

4 tablespoons bread crumbs
4 tablespoons grated Parmesan
    cheese
2 teaspoons dried sweet basil
Salt and pepper
12 small, well shaped tomatoes

Mix bread crumbs, grated Parmesan, basil, and salt and pepper to taste. Carve the stem out of the top of each tomato so there is a nice little gully to hold the crumb mixture. (You can cut it in zigzags to give a nice star shape.)

Place the filled tomatoes on a flat, oven-proof dish that will just hold them and add ¾ cup of water to the dish. Put into a preheated 350° oven and bake 30 minutes.

Serves 12.

Salade d'Épinards

2 pounds raw spinach
18 radishes
1 red onion
1 teaspoon salt
1 clove garlic
4 tablespoons lemon juice
8 tablespoons olive oil
Freshly ground black pepper

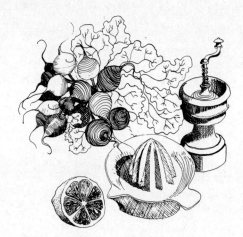

Buy unpackaged spinach so you can select tiny, tender leaves. Cut away tough stems and tear leaves in bite-size pieces. Wash very well. Dry in a towel and chill in the refrigerator. Slice radishes very thin; slice onion into paper-thin rings.

Sprinkle salt into wooden salad bowl and rub with cut garlic clove.

Discard garlic. Add lemon juice and olive oil. Add spinach, radishes and red onion. Grind black pepper over all. Toss well with spoon and fork.

Serves 12.

Strawberries Karenina

Make this early in the morning and keep covered in the refrigerator until serving time. The flavors blend together in a delightful fashion. Leave the berries whole—unless, of course, they are too large to eat gracefully. I like the sensation of biting down on a slightly crisp berry covered with smooth, creamy sauce.

3 quarts strawberries
1 quart vanilla ice milk

2 cups calorie-reduced nondairy whipped topping
½ cup Cointreau

Wash and hull berries and pat dry on paper towels. Slice large ones in half. Put into a serving bowl (reserving a few for garnish). Cover with plastic wrap and chill until needed.

Leave ice milk out of refrigerator for half an hour or so, just enough to soften a little. Work it quickly with a spoon until it is smooth and soft, then combine with the calorie-reduced whipped topping. Stir in Cointreau and blend well. Pour over berries in serving bowl and garnish with the reserved berries. Cover and hold in the refrigerator until serving time.

Serves 12.

CHAPTER THREE

Formal Sit-Down Dinners

The very best party, the most satisfactory to me as a hostess (or as a guest), is the small sit-down dinner for six or eight people. And it means that I entertain more often, with smaller groups. My mother always had parties back to back, two days in a row. Her reasoning: the silver was clean, and so was the house; the marketing for both parties was done at once; she could use the same menu; and the flowers would do for both days. The best china was kept on the top pantry shelf, so while it was down she had another party!

It is feasible to plan, buy, cook and serve a dinner party for six people without any help at all. The vital word here is "plan." Holding the guest list to four or six is step one. Take all the special pains you like, but leave time for a relaxing bath and half an hour with your feet up before the guests arrive.

Every now and again in one's life comes the need to entertain formally. Perhaps it is just the longing to put on a lovely gown and dine in style from the best china. Impending nuptials, anniversaries, visiting notables—there are lots of good excuses to have a party.

The highest compliment you can pay a friend is to invite him to share a meal at your home. This goes back to time immemorial when Joe Stoneage asked his buddy over to the cave to sample what the little woman had made of the week's hunt. There are dozens of reasons to have people to dinner; the best is just because you want to see them and feed them something good to eat. Styles in entertaining are changing, with fewer courses, more exotic foods, and all sorts of ethnic foods. The same old basic reason still applies: everyone has to eat, and it is warmer and more loving to eat together.

65

An elegant dinner party need not mean creamy, buttery food. This menu (page 71) revolves around spectacular Crown Roast of Lamb.

Several of us, last year, decided to have the fun of doing a formal dinner. All it took was planning to dine at a perfectly appointed table on superb, elegant food. The first party was so much fun it was soon followed by another, and still another. We entertained each other without extra help of any kind. We gave small dinners with never more than twelve guests, sometimes eight and usually six. When there were more than six, the food was set out on a buffet and we served ourselves, then sat down at the dining table. The hostess had a serving cart nearby and traffic back and forth to the kitchen was held to a minimum. One of the guests was asked to act as sommelier while the host carved or served.

Last New Year's Eve we gathered at the home of our friendly neighborhood psychiatrist. Dinner was served at 9 P.M. The candles were guttering in their sockets when we arose from the table at 2 A.M., wondering where the evening had gone. At midnight we had drunk champagne and everyone got up and kissed everyone else. Then we all resumed our seats and kept on talking for two hours more.

As we are all weight-conscious, the menus we planned were not heavy: four courses, including salad. A first course—hot soup in winter, cold in summer—is filling and not fattening. Any seafood, almost, is a perfect way to begin a meal. The main course with one vegetable, followed by salad and dessert, can fill up the heartiest eater and still not be too much for the miniature lady on his left. Everything depends on the size of the servings. Cooked carefully, with the cook's eye on the caloric content, we can party to our heart's content and our figure's delight.

If you are a working lady, and who of us today is not, entertain on weekends. However, if your schedule permits, small weekday dinners are most appealing. Your guests will usually take themselves off by ten or eleven, known locally as a "decent hour."

There are ways to make serving a party easier on the hostess. For example, use oven-to-table serving dishes, have the first course in place on the table before the guests arrive, or serve it in the living room as an accompaniment to cocktails. A teacart or serving table can be placed beside the hostess to hold used dishes, cutting down on trips to the kitchen. If we are having wine with dinner, I have given up using water glasses.

If flowers are out of season or might strain the budget to the breaking point, look around and find something to use instead. Figurines, an old tureen, or a bowl of shiny apples or bright yellow lemons can be used as a centerpiece.

The menus in this chapter have been planned for six people, my ideal size for a dinner party. It is easy to expand to eight, or double for twelve. You will find hints on serving food and different ways of presenting it to ease your task, and make having parties as much fun as going to them. (I *like* parties!)

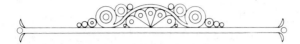

Chicken Breasts Grand Marnier for Six

Artichokes Strasbourg
Chicken Breasts Grand Marnier
Classic Green Beans
Claire's Endive and Watercress Salad
English Trifle

Everything on this menu can be prepared ahead of time. You begin with the appetizer and the dessert, which can be fixed in the morning or the day before the dinner. The salad dressing *must* be made the day before. You place the first course on the table before the guests arrive (unless the temperature is 90°). Your main course, the chicken breasts, is in the oven. Just before you sit down for dinner, nip into the kitchen for the last touch—pouring the sauce over the chicken. Then it bakes for the last 15 minutes while you are eating the first course. As it is served in the same casserole in which you cooked it, you simply place it on the buffet or in front of the host for serving. The green beans reheat while you are eating the first course; the salad is already dressed. If you have a teacart, place the used dishes out of sight on the bottom shelf. Have your dessert in position on the sideboard (unless, again, the weather is terribly hot). Have the coffee ready in an electric percolator that keeps it at perfect serving temperature until you want it.

Serve coffee wherever it suits your mood. We like to linger with our coffee in the dining room, but others prefer to move into the living room, away from the littered dining table. For the past five years I have served nothing but caffeine-reduced coffee. I use ground coffee (not instant) and make it in a drip pot, or an Italian espresso maker. Demitasse or large cups—once again, it is your personal choice. Have milk, sugar, and sugar substitute available for those who want them.

Artichokes Strasbourg

Prepare these in the morning, or the day before. Artichoke bottoms can be bought in cans or jars. People who love fresh artichokes can cook them from scratch, reserving the bottoms for this recipe—and eat up all the rest themselves!

2   16-ounce cans artichoke bottoms
    (or 12 fresh artichokes)
2   tablespoons butter
½ pound chicken livers
½ cup onions, finely chopped
½ pound fresh mushrooms, sliced
½ cup sherry
Salt and pepper to taste
Parsley or watercress for garnish

Canned artichoke bottoms need only be drained, rinsed and patted dry with paper towels.

To prepare fresh artichokes, cut ¼ inch off the tips, put artichokes in a large kettle of boiling salted water, cover, and boil until tender, 30 to 45 minutes. Drain and cool. (Pull off the leaves, wrap them in plastic wrap, and keep in the refrigerator until you want to eat them.) Discard the chokes. Reserve the bottoms.

Melt butter in Teflon pan over medium heat and sauté chicken livers, onions and mushrooms until soft and all red has disappeared from livers. Place in blender with the sherry, salt and pepper to taste and blend 2 minutes at high speed, until smooth.

Spread the chicken liver mixture neatly on artichoke bottoms. Put on a dish, cover with plastic wrap, and chill in the refrigerator until serving time. Just before guests arrive put on individual plates, garnish with sprigs of parsley or watercress, and set in place on the dining table.

Serves 6.

Chicken Breasts Grand Marnier

You can do most of this early in the day and finish the dish just before serving time. I have a Pyrex dish that fits in a silver holder, most elegant-looking.

4 tablespoons butter
6 chicken breasts (12 pieces),
    skinned and boned
1 teaspoon salt
1 teaspoon paprika
3 cups onion, finely chopped

2 tablespoons lemon juice
2 tablespoons orange juice
    concentrate, undiluted
6 tablespoons Grand Marnier (or
    other orange liqueur)

Melt the butter in Teflon pan. Sauté chicken breasts a few at a time, until all are browned. Sprinkle with salt and paprika.

Spread half the chopped onion in a lightly greased baking dish, one you can use for serving. Put the chicken breasts on top of the onions. Spread them with the remaining onions and cover with lid of aluminum foil.

Put into a preheated 350° oven and bake about 50 minutes. You can stop at this point, take it out of the oven, and let wait at room temperature for 1 or 2 hours. (If you do this early, place in the refrigerator. Then take the dish out 1 or 2 hours before cooking time to return to room temperature. Otherwise 15 minutes' cooking time will be insufficient.)

Fifteen minutes before serving, combine remaining ingredients in a bowl and beat with a wire whisk until blended. Drizzle over the chicken. Put back in preheated 350° oven and bake uncovered 15 minutes more, until bubbling hot and nicely glazed with the sauce.

Serves 6.

Classic Green Beans

Fresh beans are immeasurably better than frozen, and when you cook beans this way you have never had them so good!

2 pounds fresh green beans (or 3 9-ounce boxes frozen)
2 tablespoons butter
1 teaspoon salt

Use fresh beans, preferably, and cook them the following way. Early in the day fill the largest kettle in the house with water and bring it to a boil. Remove the ends of the beans but do not slice. Dump the beans in the water. As soon as the water comes back to a full rolling boil, time the beans for 5 minutes. Then drain the beans in a colander and run cold water over them for 3 or 4 minutes. Drain beans again and hold at room temperature until just before serving time. (If you use frozen beans cook them a minute or two less than package directions, drain and proceed as above.)

At dinner time, melt 2 tablespoons butter in a skillet, add beans, and heat over low fire, shaking pan occasionally so the beans don't scorch. Add salt, mix well, and serve.

Serves 6.

Claire's Endive and Watercress Salad

It is important that the dressing meld for 24 hours to develop flavor, so make it the day before the party. This very special dressing has a sweetness that offsets the fresh tangy greens.

½ teaspoon salt
½ teaspoon dry mustard
½ teaspoon poppy seeds
¼ cup vinegar
¼ cup sugar
½ cup salad oil
2   bunches watercress
6   heads Belgian endive

The day before the party, make the dressing: place salt, mustard, poppy seeds, vinegar and sugar in blender. Blend at low speed for 1 minute. With the blender still running at low speed, slowly pour in salad oil and blend until all is in. This dressing has the consistency of mayonnaise. Store in a covered jar in the refrigerator.

Wash watercress and shake dry. Remove stems. Slice endive across in ¼-inch rounds, and separate. Place greens in a salad bowl, cover with plastic wrap, and chill in refrigerator until needed.

At serving time shake dressing vigorously, pour over greens and toss well. Serve at once.

Serves 6.

English Trifle

2-ounce package (2 envelopes)
    calorie-reduced vanilla
    pudding
4 cups skim milk for the pudding
6 ladyfingers
½ cup calorie-reduced strawberry
    jam
¼ cup cream sherry
1 tablespoon walnuts, chopped
16-ounce can calorie-reduced pear
    halves (about 6 halves)

Make the pudding with the milk as directed on the package. Cool.

Split the ladyfingers and spread with the jam. Cut the ladyfingers in half crossways and place 4 pieces in each dessert dish, jam side up (or use a crystal serving dish and place all the ladyfingers in a layer at the bottom).

Spoon the sherry over the ladyfingers. Sprinkle with the chopped walnuts. Cut the pears into small pieces and spread on top of the walnuts.

Beat the cooled pudding well and spoon over the pears. Cover with plastic wrap and chill for at least 3 hours.

Serves 6.

Variation:

Use apricot jam and 1 8-ounce can of calorie-reduced mandarin oranges (drained) instead of pears.

Crown Roast of Lamb for Six

Seafood Aspic
Crown Roast of Lamb Bombay Style
Purée of Peas in Onion Cups
Grapefruit and Chicory with Fruit Salad Dressing
Mocha Pot de Crème

This is a very fancy dinner, yet it is not difficult to prepare. Order the crown roast from your butcher well in advance so he has time to trim the fat off and tie it up properly. Be very sure that he removes all the fat before he grinds the meat he takes from the bones. You will use this ground meat in the stuffing for the roast. Only a very loving butcher will prepare this fabulous-looking roast, so start cultivating him ahead of time. Don't expect to waltz into the shop at 4 P.M. and have him be overjoyed at your order.

The first course and dessert should be prepared the day before the party.

Seafood Aspic

2 bouillon cubes, beef or chicken
½ cup boiling water
2 envelopes unflavored gelatin
¼ cup cold water
2 cups V-8 juice
2 tablespoons lemon juice
½ teaspoon salt
2 7-ounce cans crabmeat
½ green pepper, finely chopped
Parsley sprigs
3 lemons, thinly sliced, for
    garnish
Parsley, finely chopped, for
    garnish

Dissolve the bouillon cubes in ½ cup boiling water. Soften the gelatin in ¼ cup cold water, put into a saucepan, and dissolve over low heat. Combine the bouillon, gelatin, V-8 juice, lemon juice and salt. Chill until it begins to thicken.

Meanwhile, rinse crabmeat very well in cold water. Pick over crabmeat, discarding any shell and cartilage. Flake and combine the crabmeat with the thickened gelatin mixture and stir in the green pepper. Pour into lightly oiled 1-quart mold. Chill until firm. Unmold (as directed on page 117).

Fill the center with parsley sprigs. Surround with overlapping lemon slices. Sprinkle lightly with chopped parsley and serve.

Serves 6.

Crown Roast of Lamb Bombay Style

This is a striking main course and an easy one to carve in case you are married to an ungifted amateur.

1 pound lentils
3 tablespoons butter
3 large onions, finely chopped
¼ teaspoon turmeric
¼ teaspoon pepper
½ teaspoon allspice
1 large apple, peeled, cored, and
      chopped
1 teaspoon salt
16-rib crown roast of lamb, prepared
      by butcher
Salt and pepper to season lamb
Watercress for garnish

Put lentils into a kettle with salted water to cover, bring to a boil, and simmer until tender (about 30 minutes). Drain lentils and reserve liquid.

Melt butter in Teflon pan, sauté onion until brown, and add turmeric, pepper and allspice. Stir well. Add the chopped apple and cook until apple is tender. Salt, and add ground meat which the butcher has removed from the lamb ribs. Cook a few minutes more, until ground lamb has taken on a little color. Then put into a large bowl and mix in drained lentils—do this lightly so lentils won't squash.

Take the crown of lamb out of the refrigerator in time to come to room temperature by roasting time. Twist a little hat of aluminum foil around each exposed rib. Put into a roasting pan and fill center of crown with the lentil mixture.

Put into a preheated 450° oven for 30 minutes, then remove from oven and spoon off accumulated fat, or siphon it off with a bulb baster. Reduce heat to 350°. Check filling at this point—if it is too dry, moisten it with a few spoonfuls of the hot, reserved lentil liquid. Roast 2½ hours longer for well done, or 2 hours if you like it still pink.

Take out of oven, place on a handsome platter or carving board, and let sit for 20 minutes before carving. Remove the protective foil from ribs and replace with paper frills.

At serving time, surround with Purée of Peas in Onion Cups and garnish with watercress.

Serves 6 to 8.

Purée of Peas in Onion Cups

3 pounds fresh peas (or 3-9 ounce
      packages frozen)
6 large Bermuda onions
1 teaspoon salt
4 tablespoons calorie-reduced sour
      cream
Pepper to taste

Shell the peas and cook them until tender, then push them through a fine sieve. (This is sort of a bore, but it's one job the blender can't do right.) Set puréed peas aside.

Cook the *unpeeled* onions in boiling water until just tender. Onions vary, so you have to gauge the tenderness when boiling them; if they're too well done they have a terrible tendency to collapse. Drain and set aside until cool enough to handle. Onion cups are simple to make when onion is cooked: the outer skins slip off easily, and the centers pull out with no trouble. Leave a shell about ½-inch thick.

Mix the puréed peas with salt and sour cream, add pepper to taste, mix well, and stuff into onions.

Set stuffed onions into a flat, rimmed baking dish and put into the hot 350° oven when you take out the crown roast of lamb. Leave onions in 20 minutes, just long enough to gild the tops and heat them through.

Place on the platter around the crown roast of lamb.

Serves 6.

Grapefruit and Chicory with Fruit Salad Dressing

1 recipe Fruit Salad Dressing (page 188)
3 large seedless grapefruit, pink or white
Chicory

Make the Fruit Salad Dressing.
Peel and section the grapefruit.

Place some crisp chicory (that's the curly kind) on individual plates and arrange 4 or 5 sections of grapefruit on each.

Shake dressing well and spoon about 1 tablespoon over fruit on each serving.

Serves 6.

Mocha Pot de Crème

2-ounce package (2 envelopes) calorie-reduced chocolate pudding
3 cups strong coffee
1 cup skim milk
6 tablespoons calorie-reduced nondairy whipped topping

Make the pudding, following the package directions, using the coffee and milk (instead of all milk).

When done, pour into little chocolate pots and let chill. When cold, top with a spoonful of whipped topping and refrigerate until ready to serve.

Serves 6.

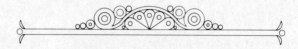

Tenderloin of Beef for Eight

Tomato Madrilène
Roast Tenderloin of Beef
Beets with Horseradish
Broccoli Maître d'Hôtel
Mixed Green Salad with Blue Cheese Dressing
Meringue Glacé

Here is another menu suitable for any season, elegant in appearance and simple to prepare. As you need to buy a whole tenderloin, consider stretching your guest list to eight. Tenderloin *is* expensive, but remember you are not paying for bone, fat and gristle, only for the most tender, delicious meat. You should order the tenderloin in advance from your butcher.

Tomato Madrilène

3 13-ounce cans tomato
    madrilène
3 tablespoons dry sherry
1 envelope unflavored gelatin
¼ cup cold water

Empty the cans of tomato madrilène into a saucepan and heat gently just until hot. (Do not boil.)

Stir in the sherry. Soak the gelatin in the cold water until softened, then stir into the hot soup until dissolved. At once pour to a depth of 1 inch into 2 8-inch-square pans and refrigerate until very firm. At serving time, cut into 1-inch squares and pile into chilled shallow soup cups.
Serves 8.

Roast Tenderloin of Beef

This is simple and quick to do, tastes incredibly good, and appeals to everyone.

1 tenderloin of beef, 7 or 8 pounds, all fat removed
1 clove garlic, halved
Salt and pepper
Watercress (or parsley) **sprigs to garnish**

Trim the tenderloin to remove as much fat as possible, if the butcher has not done this for you. Preheat oven to 500°. Place meat on roasting pan. Rub surface of meat with cut garlic clove and season well with salt and pepper.

Put into the oven and roast 25 to 30 minutes for rare, 30 to 35 minutes for medium rare, and 40 to 45 minutes for well done.

Remove from oven and place on wooden board. Cut into 1-inch slices, slightly on the diagonal. Surround the meat with Beets with Horseradish and garnish with watercress sprigs.

Serves 8.

Beets with Horseradish

These beets are bright and beautiful in looks and taste.

16-ounce can or jar deluxe tiny whole beets
2-ounce jar prepared horseradish

Drain the beets and pat dry with paper towels. With a sharp little knife carve a small hole in the top of each beet. Put a little dab of horseradish in each. Cover with plastic wrap and place in the refrigerator until time to serve on the meat platter.

Serves 8.

Broccoli Mâitre d'Hôtel

1 large bunch fresh broccoli (or 3 10-ounce packages frozen spears)
1 tablespoon butter
½ cup seasoned bread crumbs
Juice of 1 lemon

Trim and cut fresh broccoli into spears, peeling the stems with a vegetable peeler. Cook uncovered for 12 to 15 minutes in boiling salted water —until just tender. Do not overcook. Drain well. If using frozen broccoli, cook according to package directions and drain well. Place drained broccoli in a rimmed serving dish and keep warm.

Melt the butter in a small Teflon pan. Stir in crumbs, cook for a moment, and add lemon juice. Spoon over broccoli and serve at once.

Serves 8.

Mixed Green Salad with Blue Cheese Dressing

Vary the salad greens according to what is available on the market. Don't always have the same kind of lettuce.

1   recipe Blue Cheese Dressing
     (page 189)
1   head romaine
1   head chicory
1   head endive
1   bunch watercress
¼ pound blue cheese, crumbled

Make the Blue Cheese Dressing. Wash the greens and shake to dry. (Use paper towels if necessary.) Tear the greens into bite-size pieces— *never* cut greens with a knife. Arrange in a large salad bowl and keep in the refrigerator.

At serving time, dress with the Blue Cheese Dressing, toss well, and strew the crumbled blue cheese on top. Serve at once.

Serves 8.

Meringue Glacé

It is unbelievable the mileage you get from two egg whites! Here is a classic dessert, usually considered very fattening. I have fixed it so it's not.

2   egg whites (at room temperature)
½ cup (8 tablespoons) superfine
     sugar
½ teaspoon vanilla
1   pint vanilla ice milk
6-ounce can calorie-reduced
     chocolate syrup (see Appendix)

Beat 2 egg whites until very stiff and dry. Beat in 6 tablespoons sugar, adding a spoonful at a time. Continue beating until the mixture holds its shape. Add ½ teaspoon vanilla. Fold in the remaining 2 tablespoons of sugar, continuing to beat for another few minutes.

Cover a cookie sheet with plain, unwaxed paper. (You can cut open a brown paper bag to fit.) Shape the meringue with a spoon or pastry bag into 16 oval shapes. Bake 45 to 60 minutes in a preheated 225° oven. Remove meringues from paper. (If they stick to the paper, wipe the back of the paper with a damp cloth.)

While the meringues are still warm, crush the flat side with your thumb and remove the soft center with a teaspoon.

At serving time, fill the hollowed shells with ice milk. Place two filled meringues together, on a dessert plate. Top with 2 tablespoons calorie-reduced chocolate syrup.

Serves 8.

Savory Veal Pot Roast for Six

Stuffed Artichokes
Savory Veal Pot Roast
Green Mountain Onions
Asparagus Polonaise
Lemon Mousse à l'Orange

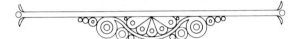

At your formal dinners you want to serve with all the elegance at your command. It is the little things that count. In this menu, for example, garnishing the roast with sprigs of watercress or parsley adds color and crispness. Contrasts in texture and color are important in every meal you serve. Here the orange shells holding the lemon mousse on shiny green leaves are doubly appealing since they look so beautiful and are low-calorie, too!

Stuffed Artichokes

These are equally good hot, warm or at room temperature.

6   well-shaped artichokes
1   clove garlic
½ pound cooked shrimp
5-ounce can water chestnuts,
     drained
2   tablespoons olive oil
2   tablespoons flavored bread
     crumbs
½ cup white wine
Salt and pepper to taste

Soak the artichokes in salted water 1 hour. Drain. Cut the points off the leaves and level the bottoms so artichokes will sit firmly. Pry open the tops, dig out the chokes and discard.

Rub each artichoke with cut garlic clove.

Chop the shrimp and drained water chestnuts into a small mince and mix with the olive oil and bread crumbs. Divide this stuffing among the artichokes, pushing it down in the centers and among the leaves, prying them apart to get the stuffing in. Place the artichokes in a casserole, dribble white wine over them, and season well with salt and pepper.

Cover and cook over medium heat for 45 minutes to an hour, until fork tender.

Serves 6.

Savory Veal Pot Roast

Marinate meat overnight for this good dish.

1 recipe Oil and Lemon Dressing
        (page 189)
6- or 7-pound rolled loin of veal
1 clove garlic
1 teaspoon salt
¼ teaspoon pepper
1 teaspoon oregano
2 tablespoons olive oil
3 onions, sliced thin
3 celery stalks, sliced in thin
        rounds
1 cup Fat-free Chicken Bouillon
        (page 192 or 193)
6 small carrots
½ pound fresh button mushrooms
        (or 4½-ounce can)
½ cup dry white wine
Watercress or parsley to garnish

Make Oil and Lemon Dressing.

Rub veal all over with cut clove of garlic. Cut a piece of cheesecloth large enough to cover the veal, and soak cloth in salad dressing. Wrap the veal in the cheesecloth, put in a plastic bag, and place in refrigerator overnight. Before cooking, remove veal from refrigerator, unwrap, and let stand at room temperature 1 hour. Rub well with salt, pepper and oregano.

Heat oil in a Dutch oven. Add onions and celery and sauté until limp. Put veal on top of onions and celery. Pour hot chicken bouillon around (not over) veal. Cover and simmer over low heat until tender, about 4 hours. (Or you can put it in a preheated 275° oven for the same time.) If it seems dry during cooking, add a little hot water.

Half an hour before it is done, add carrots. Twenty minutes later, add mushrooms and wine and simmer 10 minutes more. Remove veal to hot platter. Surround with carrots and mushrooms and garnish with parsley or watercress sprigs. Spoon sauce over all, and serve.

Serves 6.

Green Mountain Onions

3 cups Fat-free Chicken Bouillon
        (page 192 or 193)
18 small white onions, peeled
2 tablespoons calorie-reduced
        maple syrup
1 tablespoon Worcestershire sauce

Make chicken bouillon.

Put in a saucepan with the rest of the ingredients and cook, uncovered, over low heat, stirring occasionally, 20 or 30 minutes, until the onions are tender and the sauce almost absorbed.

Serves 6.

Asparagus Polonaise

3 10-ounce packages jumbo frozen
   asparagus spears
1 tablespoon melted butter
1 tablespoon lemon juice
2 tablespoons butter
1 cup dry bread crumbs
1 hard-cooked egg, chopped fine
¼ teaspoon salt
¼ teaspoon pepper

Cook asparagus according to package directions. Drain very well, using paper towels to absorb all moisture. Place on hot serving dish (not silver). Brush with 1 tablespoon melted butter mixed with lemon juice.

To make Polonaise sauce, melt 2 tablespoons butter in saucepan, add bread crumbs, and sauté until lightly brown. Watch this like a hawk for the crumbs can burn in a second. Remove from heat, mix in chopped egg, salt and pepper. Sprinkle Polonaise sauce over asparagus and serve at once.

Serves 6.

Lemon Mousse à l'Orange

Beautiful oranges are easy to find in midwinter, so choose attractive ones —they will appear on the table.

2 envelopes unflavored gelatin
4 tablespoons cold water
½ cup superfine sugar
Grated rind of 3 lemons
Juice of 3 lemons
½ cup Marsala wine
8 eggs, separated
6 large navel oranges

Soak the gelatin in the cold water to soften.

Mix the sugar, grated rind, lemon juice and wine in the top of a double boiler and stir over hot, not boiling, water. When this mixture is hot, add the softened gelatin and stir until gelatin is dissolved.

Beat egg yolks until thick and lemon colored, and stir into the lemon-gelatin mixture. Beat egg whites until stiff, then fold them in gently, too. Place in refrigerator until firm, but still light and foamy, about 2 hours.

Meanwhile, hollow out the oranges. Cut an inch off the stem end. Working with a sharp, pointed knife, scoop out as much of the pulp as you can without cutting through the outer skin. (Save the pulp for tomorrow's breakfast.)

Prop the orange shells in a muffin tin and pile each one high with the lemon mousse. Return to refrigerator until serving time.

Serve on pretty green leaves on your best dessert plates.

Serves 6.

Rock Cornish Hens for Six

Greek Lemon Soup
Rock Cornish Hens with Dorrie's Stuffing
Herbed Green Beans
Iceberg Wedges with Watercress Dressing
Fabulous Fruits Flambée

Try to find small Cornish hens. The large ones are just too much food for one person, yet it looks chintzy to cut them in half.

The Fruits Flambée is a fantastic dessert—each person cooks his own fruit on a fondue fork, in a mixture of rum and liqueur set aflame in the center of the table.

Greek Lemon Soup

6 cups Fat-free Chicken Bouillon
    (page 192 or 193)
¼ cup raw rice
3 eggs, beaten
Juice of 3 large lemons

Make Fat-free Chicken Bouillon. Heat it to boiling, add rice (*not* instant rice), cover, and cook over low flame 20 minutes. Beat eggs with beater until frothy, then beat in lemon juice.

Dip out a cupful of the simmering chicken bouillon and *very slowly* add it to the beaten egg, stirring constantly. Take the chicken bouillon and rice off the fire, and little by little add to it the beaten egg and bouillon, stirring constantly until blended. Pour into individual soup cups and serve at once.

Serves 6.

Rock Cornish Hens with Dorrie's Stuffing

6   stalks celery, finely chopped
2   medium onions, finely chopped
3   4½-ounce cans mushrooms,
       coarsely chopped
12 pieces Melba toast, crumbled
4   tablespoons melted butter
½   cup port wine
1   egg, beaten
1   cup small seedless white grapes
       (optional)
6   1- to 1½-pound Rock Cornish
       hens
Salt and pepper
4   tablespoons softened butter
Watercress sprigs (or parsley) for
       garnish

For the stuffing, combine first 8 ingredients and mix together lightly. This can be done in advance and refrigerated until time to stuff birds.

Wash the hens inside and out and pat dry with paper towels. Sprinkle cavities with salt and fill loosely with the stuffing (do not pack tightly). Truss legs and wings close to body.

Spread birds with 4 tablespoons softened butter and salt and pepper generously. Place breasts up in a roasting pan. (Use two that will fit in your oven if you haven't one large enough.)

Put into a preheated 375° oven and roast, uncovered, 1 to 1¼ hours, basting with the drippings every 10 minutes—it is the basting that keeps the hens moist and delicious.

Put hens onto a large, rimmed platter, garnish with clumps of watercress and serve with a flourish.

Serves 6.

Herbed Green Beans

2   pounds fresh green beans (or 3
       10-ounce packages frozen)
2   tablespoons butter
2   medium onions, finely chopped
6-inch celery stalk, finely chopped
1   clove garlic, pressed
¼   cup parsley, finely chopped
¼   teaspoon dried rosemary
¼   teaspoon dried dillweed
Salt to taste

Cook fresh green beans as directed on page 69, omitting butter.

For the herb sauce, melt butter in Teflon pan and add chopped onions, celery and garlic. Sauté 5 minutes until limp and golden. Add parsley and herbs, and salt to taste. Simmer, covered, 10 minutes. This can wait at room temperature until dinner time.

When your beans are heated up and ready to serve, pour in the hot sautéed herb sauce, mix well, and bring to the table in a deep, rimmed vegetable dish.

Serves 6.

Iceberg Wedges with Watercress Dressing

Sometimes it is very hard to find any lettuce except iceberg in the market. Especially in autumn and winter when you want a salad, iceberg is the only answer. But you'll find it particularly good with this dressing.

1 recipe Oil and Vinegar Dressing (page 189)
⅓ cup watercress leaves, chopped (or parsley)
1 large head iceberg lettuce

Make the Oil and Vinegar Dressing, and add watercress.

Wash lettuce under running cold water, drain and pat dry with paper towels. Cut head of lettuce into 6 wedges (this is the only time you ever cut greens). Place on individual salad plates and spoon dressing over them just before serving. Use the remaining watercress to garnish the platter with the Cornish hens.

Serves 6.

Fabulous Fruits Flambée

This dessert is a dazzler! When you set fire to liqueurs, most of the calories go up in smoke—would that it were so easy with other foods! Melons, peaches, apricots, bananas, grapes, pineapples, and cherries can be used, all are good, in any combination. You may have to refill the liqueur bowl because this dessert will go on as long as there is any fruit left to be flambéed.

Assorted fresh fruit, cut as needed, about 1 cupful per person
⅔ cup 151-proof Demerara rum
⅓ cup orange liqueur
Fresh mint sprigs

Take a large, shallow bowl and fill with cracked ice. Sink a metal container—stainless steel, silver, or even a tin can if you have nothing else—in the ice. The container should hold at least 1 cup. Place bowl in freezer to get ice very hard.

Cut fruit in advance. (Cantaloupes can be cut in small wedges, other melons in balls; peaches should be peeled and cut in half; bananas cut in ½-inch diagonal slices; grapes left in small clusters.) Cover fruit with plastic wrap and keep chilled until serving time.

At serving time, arrange the fruit on the ice around the container. Garnish with sprigs of fresh mint. If all the fruit won't fit on the ice, place individual bowls of assorted fruit before each guest.

Warm rum and orange liqueur, pour into metal container, and set aflame. Each guest is given a plate, a fondue fork and a small fruit knife, and selects whatever fruit he wishes. He cuts it as suits him, then spears a piece of fruit on the fork and cooks it in the flaming liqueur.

Serves 6.

Filet Mignon au Poivre for Four

Claret Consommé
Filet Mignon au Poivre
Mushrooms Flambée
Glazed Carrots
Caesar Salad
Pineapple and Strawberries au Kirsch

There are very special times when you and your husband want to have an intimate formal dinner with just your very closest friends—perhaps to toast one of your birthdays or anniversaries. This is one of the most festive and delicious menus you can imagine—and it's truly one of the fastest to prepare in the whole book. You'll be pretty busy for about ten minutes, but then it's all over. (Start the mushrooms first; they take a little longer to cook than the steak and carrots.) Just double the recipes if you decide to celebrate with eight. Champagne all the way, of course!

Claret Consommé

If yours is a winter party you may serve this consommé hot; it's equally delish.

2 14-ounce cans consommé madrilène
4 tablespoons claret
4 orange slices

Heat the consommé with the claret. Pour to the depth of 1 inch into 2 8-inch-square pans and chill overnight. At serving time cut the consommé into squares and heap into cups. Garnish each with a twisted orange slice.

Serves 4.

Filet Mignon au Poivre

2 tablespoons peppercorns, crushed
4 filet mignons, 1 inch thick
1 teaspoon salt
1 teaspoon oil
1 teaspoon butter
3 ounces brandy
½ teaspoon prepared mustard
½ teaspoon Worcestershire sauce
Watercress (or parsley) for garnish

Using a rolling-pin, crush peppercorns coarsely. Trim filets of all fat, sprinkle with salt, and lightly press the crushed peppercorns into them on both sides.

Heat oil and butter in a Teflon-lined skillet and briskly sauté steaks 2 minutes on each side. Remove steaks to heated platter and keep hot.

To the pan juices add brandy, mustard and Worcestershire sauce. Put over moderate flame, stirring, until sauce bubbles. Pour sauce over steak.

Surround steak with Mushrooms Flambée and Glazed Carrots, and garnish platter with watercress (or parsley).
Serves 4.

Mushrooms Flambée

If you really like mushrooms, prepare a lot—they are phenomenally low in calories.

1 pound medium-size mushrooms
2 tablespoons butter
Salt and pepper to taste
4 tablespoons warm brandy

Wipe mushrooms with a towel and break off stems. Melt butter in a Teflon-lined skillet. Add mushrooms and season well with salt and pepper. Sauté over medium heat, shaking the pan now and then to coat the mushrooms well with the butter. They will be limp and golden when done (about 10 to 15 minutes).

Just before serving, when Filet Mignon au Poivre and Glazed Carrots are ready, pour warm brandy over the mushrooms and set alight. When the flames die, pour the mushrooms and the resulting sauce onto one side of the steak platter.
Serves 4.

Glazed Carrots

These little gems certainly make the platter glow.

4 teaspoons butter
2 tablespoons calorie-reduced maple syrup

2 8-ounce cans tiny whole carrots, drained
Parsley, finely chopped

Melt butter in a small saucepan, add calorie-reduced maple syrup, and place the drained carrots in it. Keep moving and shaking the pan until the carrots are well coated. Sprinkle with parsley and shake some more. These really don't have to be cooked, just heated through.

Place on one side of the steak platter.

Serves 4.

Caesar Salad

If you wish, you can make your salad right at the table, just like the waiter in the fanciest restaurant. Have all your ingredients assembled neatly on a tray and you won't have to go dashing back and forth to the pantry.

2 heads romaine lettuce
1 garlic clove, pressed
Salt
8 anchovies
4 tablespoons olive oil
Juice of 2 lemons
Freshly ground black pepper
2 eggs, coddled
2 thin slices of toast, cut in ½-inch
cubes

Wash romaine, pat dry, put into plastic bag and chill until serving time.

Place garlic, salt and anchovies in the bottom of your salad bowl. Grind them all to a paste with the back of a spoon, and add oil and lemon juice, blending well. Grind in pepper to taste.

Coddle eggs as follows: put eggs in shells in boiling water for 1 minute. Remove. Toast 2 slices of thin bread and cut into cubes.

At serving time, break romaine in bite-size pieces and add to salad bowl. Break coddled eggs into bowl and toss well, at least 30 times. Just before serving add toast cubes and toss again.

Serves 4.

Pineapple and Strawberries au Kirsch

Have the dessert all assembled on dessert plates, chilling in the refrigerator. It couldn't be simpler.

2 pints fresh strawberries
1 large ripe pineapple
4 tablespoons kirsch
Fresh mint for garnish

Wash strawberries, hull, and pat dry with paper towels. Slice pineapple in ¾-inch rounds, core and cut off rind. Place a center slice on each dessert plate.

Put the largest, handsomest strawberries in a circle on top, sprinkle with kirsch and garnish with mint sprigs. Cover with plastic wrap and chill until needed.

Serves 4.

CHAPTER FOUR

Informal Sit-Down Dinners

Happiness is having a few friends in for dinner. The menus in this chapter are more informal than those in Chapter Three. They are fancier than home-style fare, suitable for serving before an evening of cards, as a welcome to a returning student, or when one of the youngsters has a friend to "sleep over." Ask the new neighbors over for a meal with the people from the house on the other side. Share the warmth of your fireside with an acquaintance—it might lead to an expanded relationship.

Some of the best dinner parties are almost impromptu gatherings of a few congenial souls around a kitchen table. Maria called the week before and asked if we were going to Katherine's cocktail bash. When I said yes, she asked us to come home to supper with them afterward. We had Beef Fondue with Asparagus Vinaigrette, followed by Bananas Flambée in their candlelit kitchen, and several hours of delightful talk.

The table setting for these parties is always simple; a flowered cloth with pottery dishes, or copper serving platters instead of silver. Use a beautiful houseplant for a centerpiece; it can go back to its place in the window after dinner. No house plant? A bowl of fruit, shiny apples, or a pile of oranges and lemons will fill the bill.

These dinners were designed as sit-down meals, because I find it impossible to cope with chicken, duckling, or a veal knuckle on a plate on my lap. Even the smallest efficiency apartment has room for a folding table of some sort that can be pressed into service as a dining table. A card table with a removable plywood circle top seats six nicely.

I have included a low-budget meal; we all have those days when we must stretch the pennies but still want to entertain. Many of the recipes can be prepared the day before the party, a help to the working wife or busy

A low-calorie favorite, fish is the mainstay of Kona Coast, Hawaii Dinner (page 98), which also stars mushrooms, zucchini, cucumbers, pineapple.

volunteer. I have offered a wide variety of food in this chapter. Often we fall into a rut, serving the same meals repeatedly, boring ourselves and our guests. Different combinations of commonplace foods can make meals more interesting. Chicken with lobster becomes very exotic, much different from either one served by itself. Frozen duckling, which is widely available, is another good thing too rarely served at home. Several classic recipes have also been included. They have been calorie-reduced but retain all the flavor.

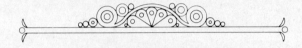

Any-time-of-year Dinner for Eight

Cucumbers Ahoy
Shish Kabob
Vegetable Medley
Peach Custard

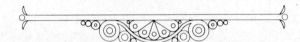

This makes an awfully nice dinner for some special, yet informal, occasion—any time of year. In winter, shish kabob does beautifully indoors on your kitchen broiler. When warm weather beckons, move the party outside and do it on the barbecue grill or hibachi.

Cucumbers Ahoy

1   recipe Oil and Lemon Dressing (page 189)
4   large cucumbers
1   pound shrimp, cooked, peeled and deveined
1   cup tomatoes, fresh or canned, drained and chopped
½   teaspoon salt
¼   teaspoon black pepper
2   scallions, finely chopped
1   cup celery, finely chopped
1   tablespoon parsley, finely chopped
3   sweet green peppers

Make Oil and Lemon Dressing.

Peel cucumbers and slice in half lengthwise. Scoop out seeds, leaving hollows. Combine shrimp with salad dressing and all remaining ingredients except green peppers and toss well. Fill the cucumber hollows with the shrimp mixture.

Cut each green pepper in three triangles (you will use 8). Spear each pepper triangle on a toothpick and stick into cucumber boats to serve as sail.

Serves 8.

Shish Kabob

4- to 5-pound leg of lamb, cut in
    2-inch cubes
1 cup dry red wine
2 medium onions, finely minced
3 garlic cloves, pressed
½ cup olive oil
1 teaspoon dried mint leaves
1 teaspoon dried marjoram
½ teaspoon freshly ground black
    pepper
1 teaspoon salt
4 large green peppers, cut in
    squares
2 tomatoes, quartered
½ pound large mushrooms

Remove any visible fat and cut meat in cubes. Combine red wine, onions, garlic, oil, mint leaves, marjoram, pepper and salt in a bowl (not metal). Mix the meat into the wine mixture, being sure each piece is coated. Marinate, covered, in the refrigerator 3 hours or more.

Clean green peppers of seeds and white membrane and cut each into 4 sections. Quarter the tomatoes. Gently wipe mushrooms and cut into thick (¼-inch) slices, right down through stems.

Remove meat from marinade with slotted spoon. Place peppers, tomatoes and mushrooms in marinade for a few minutes to coat them well. Thread meat on flat-sided skewers, alternating meat cubes with slices of pepper, tomato and mushroom.

Broil in a preheated broiler about 3 inches from heat, turning frequently so that meat browns on all sides, about 15 minutes altogether. Serve at once.

Serves 8.

Vegetable Medley

Prepare in the morning.

16-ounce can kidney beans
3 zucchini, about 7 inches long
1 pound mushrooms
2 recipes Oil and Lemon Dressing
    (page 189)
8 cupped lettuce leaves
8-ounce can pitted black olives
2 hard-cooked eggs, quartered
Chopped parsley

Drain kidney beans, discarding liquid. Slice zucchini and mushrooms. Make Oil and Lemon Dressing. Put into a bowl (not metal) and marinate the vegetables in it for at least 1 hour.

At serving time, place lettuce cups on a large platter, fill each cup with the marinated vegetables, and top with black olives and quartered eggs. Sprinkle with chopped parsley.

Serves 8.

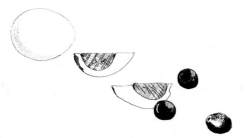

Peach Custard

2 16-ounce cans low-calorie peach
　halves, drained
1 ⅝-ounce package (2 envelopes)
　low-calorie vanilla pudding
5 cups skim milk (for the pudding)
Nutmeg

Divide drained peach halves among 8 sherbet glasses. Make the vanilla pudding as directed on the package, adding 1 cup extra milk to make it thinner and more saucy.

Pour hot pudding over peach halves and sprinkle each serving with nutmeg. Cover at once with plastic wrap and place in the refrigerator until serving time.

Serves 8.

Pantry Shelf Dinner for Six

Jellied Chicken Consommé
Salmon-broccoli Casserole
Baked Tomatoes
Pantry Shelf Salad
Poire Belle Hélène

This is called a "pantry shelf dinner" because you can keep everything needed on your pantry shelf or in your freezer—it's always there for unexpected guests. Once again, all preparations can be done some time ahead of the party.

Jellied Chicken Consommé

If the night of the party is stormy and cold, heat up the consommé and add a dash of lemon juice to each serving.

6　cups Fat-free Chicken Bouillon
　　(page 192 or 193)
3　envelopes unflavored gelatin
½　cup cold water

Dash of Tabasco
6　lemon quarters
Chopped parsley to garnish

Make Fat-free Chicken Bouillon and add gelatin to it as follows: soak gelatin in ½ cup cold water to soften. Add softened gelatin to the hot bouillon and stir until dissolved. Add Tabasco. Stir well. Pour into 6 consommé cups and chill until firm. Cut lightly with a fork before serving to break up the jelly.

Serve with lemon quarters and chopped parsley to garnish.

Serves 6.

Salmon-broccoli Casserole

3   10-ounce packages frozen broccoli spears, cooked
6   salmon steaks, fresh or frozen
2   8-ounce cans calorie-reduced condensed mushroom soup
1   cup bottled calorie-reduced mayonnaise (see Appendix)
2   tablespoons lemon juice
2   teaspoons salt
½   teaspoon white pepper
4   ounces sharp yellow cheese, grated
Flavored bread crumbs

Cook broccoli spears according to package directions, drain, and pat dry with paper towels.

Lightly grease a large, shallow baking dish, one you can bring to the table. Place the broccoli spears in the dish and cover each 2 or 3 spears with a salmon steak. Combine mushroom soup, mayonnaise, lemon juice, salt and pepper, and spoon over the salmon and broccoli. Sprinkle with the grated cheese and breadcrumbs. You can assemble this in the morning, cover with plastic wrap, and hold in the refrigerator— just take it out in time to come to room temperature before cooking. (If it comes chilled straight from the refrigerator, add 10 minutes to the cooking time.)

Put into a preheated 350° oven for 30 minutes, or until browned and bubbling.

Serves 6.

Baked Tomatoes

6   firm tomatoes
½   tablespoon salt
½   teaspoon white pepper
½   tablespoon brown sugar
Celery salt

Wash tomatoes and pat dry with paper towels. Cut each tomato in half and place cut side up on a lightly oiled low-rimmed flat baking dish that later can be brought to the table. (Or use an oiled cookie sheet and later transfer to a serving dish.) Mix the remaining ingredients and sprinkle over the tomatoes.

Put into a 350° oven and bake for 30 minutes, right along with the casserole.

Keep hot over a candle warmer or on an electric hot tray.

Serves 6.

Pantry Shelf Salad

This is an excellent recipe to fix when there are no greens to be had.

1 recipe Oil and Vinegar Dressing
   (page 189)
1 egg white
16-ounce can whole green beans,
   drained
8-ounce can sliced mushrooms,
   drained
1 red onion, sliced into paper-thin
   rings
4-ounce jar pimientos, drained and
   chopped
Freshly ground black pepper

Make Oil and Vinegar Dressing and put it into a screw-top jar. Add 1 unbeaten egg white to dressing and shake vigorously to blend it well. Put the beans, mushrooms, and red onion rings into a salad bowl. Pour the salad dressing over them and toss well. Garnish with pimiento bits and grind black pepper over all. Serves 6.

Poire Belle Hélène

My greedy friend Lisl loves this dessert. Since we have all grown older (and wider) I have had to devise a way to keep on serving this, while lowering the calorie count. The only reason to tell people is if they refuse it because it's not on their diet. Then confess.

2 16-ounce cans calorie-reduced
   pear halves
1 pint vanilla ice milk
6-ounce can calorie-reduced
   chocolate syrup
   (see Appendix)

Use your best crystal dessert dishes for this. Into each one put two pear halves, place a spoonful of vanilla ice milk in each half, and cover with several spoonfuls of chocolate syrup.
Serves 6.

"Guess Who's Coming to Dinner?" for Eight

Broiled Grapefruit
Chicken and Lobster Marengo
Braised Endive
Hearts of Palm Salad
Grape Glacé Cathay

This is for when your spouse announces that he's asked his old college chum and wife to dinner on Friday. Call up your best friends and make the most of it—give them this menu, which will please them all.

You have only to broil the grapefruit and braise the endive at the last minute, so you won't miss much of what is going on in the parlor. The main dish can be prepared ahead and finished just before serving.

Broiled Grapefruit

4 fine grapefruit, halved
8 teaspoons calorie-reduced maple
    syrup
4 teaspoons butter
8 fresh strawberries (or cherries)

Halve grapefruit and section well. Place on shallow pan. Put 1 teaspoon maple syrup on each half, and dot with ½ teaspoon butter in small bits.

Place in preheated broiler for 10 minutes, or just long enough to brown. Remove to serving plates and place a strawberry or cherry in the center of each.

Serves 8.

Chicken and Lobster Marengo

8   chicken breasts (16 pieces),
        skinned and boned
Salt and pepper
2   tablespoons butter
2   tablespoons dry Vermouth
½   pound mushrooms, sliced
3   ripe tomatoes, skinned, seeded
        and coarsely chopped (or 1
        cup canned tomatoes,
        drained)
2   tablespoons flour
1½ cups Fat-free Chicken Bouillon
        (page 192 or 193)
1   bay leaf, crushed
1   tablespoon tomato paste
2   tablespoons chopped chives,
        fresh or frozen
½   teaspoon salt
⅛   teaspoon pepper
2   10-ounce packages lobster tails

Season chicken breasts with salt and pepper. Heat 2 tablespoons butter in Teflon skillet and sauté chicken breasts, a few at a time, until golden brown. Remove chicken to shallow baking pan large enough to hold the pieces of chicken in one layer. Add Vermouth to Teflon skillet, put over medium heat, and deglaze all the crusty bits—it will sizzle up and the calories will disappear as well as some of the Vermouth. Pour de-glazed skillet juices over chicken.

Cover chicken pan tightly with foil. Put into a preheated 325° oven and bake 25 or 30 minutes, or until tender. Take out of oven and keep warm.

While chicken is cooking, add mushrooms to the Teflon skillet in which you browned the chicken. Cook slowly, uncovered, for 10 minutes. Add tomatoes, blend in flour, add hot chicken bouillon, and simmer over low heat, stirring, until sauce is thickened and smooth. Add bay leaf, tomato paste, chives, salt and pepper, and simmer 15 minutes more.

While the sauce is cooking, cook lobster tails according to package directions. Cut cooked lobster meat in bite-size pieces and add to sauce. Simmer 5 minutes more. (To make ahead, brown chicken and make lobster sauce in the morning and refrigerate separately. Bake chicken in oven just before dinner, and reheat lobster sauce at the last minute. Be careful not to let it boil.)

To serve, place chicken breasts on a large, heated serving platter and top with lobster sauce.

Serves 8.

Braised Endive

8 endive heads, halved
2 tablespoons butter
1 teaspoon beef extract

¼ cup hot water
Salt and pepper

Place endive halves in Teflon-lined frying pan in one layer. Dot with the butter. Mix meat extract with hot water. Pour over endive. Cover pan tightly and simmer 20 minutes, carefully turning endive occasionally so that it is coated with liquid. (Watch carefully so that it does not stick.) Salt and pepper to taste.

Serves 8.

Variation:

Canned celery hearts or fresh celery stalks can be substitued for endive.

Hearts of Palm Salad

1 recipe Oil and Lemon Dressing
    (page 189)
1 large bunch watercress (or
    shredded lettuce)
2 12-ounce cans hearts of palm
2 or 3 pimientos, sliced

Make 1 recipe Oil and Lemon Dressing. Wash watercress and shake dry. (Or wash lettuce, pat dry and shred.) Place watercress (or lettuce) on 6 salad plates. Drain the hearts of palm and slice them lengthwise. Place 3 or 4 slices on each serving and drape with a thin ribbon of pimiento. Shake dressing well and put a spoonful over hearts of palm on each plate.

Serves 8.

Grape Glace Cathay

2 cups unsweetened grape juice
8-ounce can low-calorie mandarin
    oranges, drained
2 cups water

Combine all ingredients and mix well. Freeze to a mush in 2 ice trays. Scrape from trays into a chilled bowl. Beat well. Pour back into trays and freeze firm.

Serve in crystal dishes. If you have a grape arbor, place a grape leaf under each dish.

Serves 8.

Make-ahead Dinner for Six

Sea Fare
Brisket of Beef à la Française
Broccoli Mold with Carrots
Salad in the Round
Wine Jelly Sevilla

Every item on this menu can—nay, *must*—be prepared the day before the party. Do not put the dressing on the salad until the very last minute before serving. If you are a working girl, or just like to get everything ready beforehand, this is a great, beautiful party menu with Continental overtones.

Sea Fare

This first course may be prepared the day before, held in the refrigerator, and cooked just before serving time. Easy and yummy.

4½-ounce can shrimp, rinsed and drained
6½-ounce can crabmeat, picked over, rinsed and drained
1   cup celery, chopped
1   tablespoon onion, grated
1   cup bottled low-calorie mayonnaise (see Appendix)
2   tablespoons lemon juice
½   teaspoon salt
1   teaspoon Worcestershire sauce
6   tablespoons seasoned bread crumbs

2   tablespoons butter, melted

In a bowl, combine shrimp and crabmeat with all other ingredients except crumbs and butter. Mix well and divide among 6 individual ramekins. Mix bread crumbs with melted butter and spread on top of seafood mixture.

Put ramekins into a preheated 350° oven and bake 30 minutes. Serve at once.

Serves 6.

Brisket of Beef à la Française

Prepare this the day before.

1 tablespoon shortening
6-pound brisket of beef (first cut
1 teaspoon salt
½ teaspoon freshly ground black
    pepper
2 medium onions, sliced
2 bay leaves
2 tablespoons Worcestershire sauce
¾ cup dry red wine

Heat shortening in large Teflon skillet. Season meat with salt and pepper. Brown evenly on all sides. Remove browned meat from pan, add onions, and cook until limp. Add bay leaves, Worcestershire sauce and red wine. Boil vigorously 2 minutes. Return meat to pan, cover tightly, and simmer gently over very low heat (possibly over an asbestos pad) 3 or 4 hours, until fork tender. Check occasionally to see if there is enough liquid, turning the meat at the same time. Add a little hot water if it seems dry.

Cool meat and sauce separately. When cool, cover meat and sauce bowl tightly with plastic wrap and place in the refrigerator overnight. In the morning, remove every bit of fat from the sauce. The meat, too, will be much easier to slice when cold. Slice slightly on the bias and reheat meat in the defatted sauce before serving time.

Serves 6.

Broccoli Mold with Carrots

This is colorful and delicious.

4 10-ounce packages frozen
    chopped broccoli
¼ cup skim milk
3 eggs, lightly beaten
¼ pound aged Cheddar cheese,
    crumbled
Salt and pepper
2 16-ounce cans tiny Belgian
    carrots

Cook broccoli according to package directions. Drain well.

Put milk, eggs, and crumbled cheese in blender. Blend 1 minute at high speed. Add about ⅓ cooked broccoli and salt and pepper to taste; whirl up again for 1 minute. Add the remaining broccoli in small pieces by hand. (If you blend it all it gets too smooth; you want a little texture to this.)

Pour broccoli mixture into a lightly oiled Teflon 1-quart ring mold. Place mold in a pan of hot water, put into a preheated 350° oven and bake 45 minutes.

Meanwhile heat the carrots in their own juice; drain well.

Unmold the broccoli ring (as directed on page 39). Fill center with carrots.

Serves 6.

Salad in the Round

1 recipe Herbed Dressing
  (page 187)
2 bunches watercress
2 heads Chinese cabbage
2 red onions

Make the Herbed Dressing. Wash watercress and cabbage. Shake watercress dry. Cut cabbage across the grain in ½-inch slices, leaving slices whole. Slice red onions into thin rings and separate them.

In a large shallow bowl arrange alternate rings of cabbage, onion, and bits of watercress. Pour on the salad dressing at the table so your guests can see the pretty pattern you have made.

Serves 6.

Wine Jelly Sevilla

⅝-ounce package (2 envelopes)
  orange-flavored low-calorie
  gelatin
1 cup boiling water
2 cups orange juice
1 cup port wine
Grated rind of 1 orange
3 thin center slices of orange,
   halved

Pour 1 cup boiling water over gelatin in a 1-quart bowl. Stir well to dissolve gelatin completely. Stir in the orange juice, port wine, and grated orange rind. Pour into parfait glasses and garnish each with half an orange slice. Put into refrigerator to jell; serve chilled.

Serves 6.

Kona Coast, Hawaii Dinner for Six

Mushroom Broth
Grilled Halibut Steaks
Zucchini Florentine
Cucumber Mousse
Pineapple Crème de Menthe

Don't ask how "Florentine" got into this menu—probably off a coastal trader. You may grill your halibut over charcoal or in the oven broiler. Everything else can be prepared ahead of time. Halve and scoop out the pineapples early in the day, and add the lemon ice and crème de menthe at serving time.

Mushroom Broth

A clear, light brown soup with an authentic mushroom flavor.

2 pounds mushrooms, coarsely
    chopped
2 quarts water
3 tablespoons sweet Vermouth
1 teaspoon beef extract
Salt and pepper
6 tablespoons calorie-reduced sour
    cream
Chives or parsley, chopped, for
    garnish

Simmer mushrooms in water 1 hour. Strain. Return strained broth to low fire and stir in Vermouth, meat extract, salt and pepper. Pour into individual soup dishes. Top each with 1 tablespoon sour cream and sprinkle with chopped chives or parsley.

Serves 6.

Grilled Halibut Steaks

Grilled in this simple fashion, the steaks come out lightly browned, tender and juicy.

3 lemons, halved
3 pounds halibut (6 steaks)
Parsley, finely chopped
2 lemons, cut in wedges

About an hour before serving, cut lemons in half. Put halibut steaks in a flat, rimmed dish and squeeze half a lemon over each steak. Let sit at room temperature for an hour or so,

turning the steaks once.

When ready to cook, grill over charcoal about 20 minutes, turning once. (Or put under oven broiler, about 5 inches from flame, 15 to 20 minutes, turning once.) Sprinkle with finely chopped fresh parsley and serve on a heated platter with extra lemon wedges as a garnish.

Serves 6.

Zucchini Florentine

This wedding of two vegetables beloved of Italians looks as good as it tastes.

3   zucchini, about 8 inches long,
    uniformly thick
10-ounce package frozen chopped
    spinach
2   tablespoons flour
½ cup skim milk
Salt and pepper
¼ cup Parmesan cheese, grated

Scrub zucchini and cook whole in boiling, salted water until not quite tender (about 10 minutes). Drain. When cool enough to handle, halve lengthwise and gently scoop out centers leaving a ¼-inch shell. Reserve. Chop centers and reserve.

Cook frozen chopped spinach according to package directions and drain very well. Mix with the reserved chopped zucchini.

Blend flour and milk together in a saucepan over low heat. Add spinach-zucchini mixture. Simmer, uncovered, stirring constantly for a few minutes, until thickened.

Place the zucchini shells in a single layer in a shallow baking pan that can later come to the table. Sprinkle shells with salt and pepper. Spoon spinach mixture into shells and top with grated Parmesan cheese. Put into a preheated 350° oven and bake 15 to 20 minutes, until golden and bubbling.

Serves 6.

Cucumber Mousse

This is a rich-tasting, smooth salad.

2   envelopes unflavored gelatin
½ cup cold water
2   cups cucumber, pared, seeded
    and chopped
½ teaspoon salt
¼ teaspoon white pepper
2   cups calorie-reduced cottage
    cheese
2   tablespoons white vinegar
2   tablespoons lemon juice
3   tablespoons pimiento, chopped
Watercress or chicory sprigs

Put gelatin and water in blender and let soak for 5 minutes. Add all the rest of the ingredients except pimiento and watercress (or chicory). Turn the blender on low speed 2 minutes, then up to high for 1 minute. Stir in the chopped pimientos.

Pour into a lightly oiled 6-cup ring mold and place in refrigerator to set. Unmold (as directed on page 117) onto a round platter and fill the center with crisp sprigs of watercress or chicory.

Serves 6.

Pineapple Crème de Menthe

3 medium-size ripe pineapples
Juice of 3 limes
1 pint water-based lemon ice
12 tablespoons green crème de
 menthe

To cut pineapples, place on cutting board with foliage upright. Slice straight down through leaves, cutting pineapple in half. Remove core and scoop out pulp in bite-size pieces. Sprinkle cavities with lime juice.

Divide the lemon ice among the pineapple halves. Place a few pieces of pineapple on top of the ice. Drizzle 2 tablespoons of green crème de menthe over all, and serve.

Serves 6.

Dinner for Six on a "Waiting Night"

Bouillon Chiffonade
Carol's Coq au Vin
Grandmother Payne's Cucumber Salad
Baked Apples

One Thursday night in Dublin I remarked to my Irish friends how quiet the town seemed. "Ah, it's a waiting night." "Waiting for what?" I asked. "For pay day!" came the reply. When the exchequer is low and you have impulsively invited guests to dine, this menu fills the bill.

Bouillon Chiffonade

6 cups Fat-free Vegetable Bouillon
 (page 192 or 194)
1 small head Boston lettuce
½ bunch watercress (or parsley)

Make vegetable bouillon. Finely shred lettuce and watercress leaves (discard stems). Add to boiling bouillon and simmer for 2 minutes. Take off the fire and serve at once.

Serves 6.

Carol's Coq au Vin

Long ago, during World War II, my sister and I lived in a little house in the country. Chicken was cheap and unrationed, so we often dined on Carol's version of coq au vin.

2   chickens, skin removed, cut in
      serving pieces
1½ teaspoons salt
½   teaspoon pepper
¼   cup flour
¼   cup butter (or margarine)
2   onions, sliced
2   carrots, sliced
2   stalks celery, sliced
1   pound fresh mushrooms, sliced
½   teaspoon paprika
2   cups dry red wine
A little chicken stock (if needed)
1   tablespoon flour (if needed)

Season chicken with salt and pepper and shake in bag with flour. Melt butter in Teflon pan, put in chicken pieces, a few at a time, and brown on all sides. As they are done, remove from pan.

In same pan, sauté onion, carrots, celery and mushrooms until tender. Return chicken to pan with sautéed vegetables and add paprika and red wine. Simmer, covered, over low heat for about 1 hour. Check while cooking. If it seems dry, add a little hot chicken stock. If sauce is too thin, dissolve 1 tablespoon flour into 1 tablespoon chicken stock. Stir into sauce and simmer a few minutes, stirring, until sauce thickens.

When the chicken is tender, remove it to a hot serving dish, pour the sauce over all, and serve at once.
Serves 6.

Grandmother Payne's Cucumber Salad

This cucumber recipe goes back to unrecorded time at our house. My grandmother served cucumbers this way, crispy cold and crunchy with slivers of ice floating among the thin slices.

3 or 4 medium cucumbers
Fresh dill (or dried dill weed),
      minced fine
Salt and white pepper
1 cup white vinegar (or to cover)

Score cucumbers lengthwise with the tines of a silver dinner fork to make a pretty edging. Slice paper-thin. Place in layers in a 2-quart bowl (not metal), sprinkling each layer with minced fresh dill or dried dill weed, salt, and white pepper. Add enough white vinegar to float cucumbers. Fill the bowl with ice cubes. This can be done early in the day and kept, covered, in the refrigerator until serving time.

Drain off the liquid and add a half dozen more ice cubes at serving time. Use a pierced spoon for serving to drain off excess liquid.
Serves 6.

Baked Apples

Who needs apple pie with this rich-tasting dessert? Serve warm in cold weather, chilled in summer.

6   large Rome Beauty apples
6   tablespoons low-calorie
        marmalade
½ cup apple cider
1   cup calorie-reduced nondairy
        whipped topping
Ground cinnamon

Wash and core apples without cutting through the stem end so the filling won't fall out. Fill each cavity with 1 teaspoon low-calorie orange marmalade. Set apples in a shallow baking pan, and dribble cider over them.

Put apples into a preheated 375° oven and bake about 45 minutes, or until tender but not falling apart.

Put a dollop of low-calorie whipped topping on each apple and sprinkle lightly with cinnamon.

Serves 6.

CHAPTER FIVE

Buffet Dinners

*T*he buffet dinner is often the answer to cramped dining areas—or no dining room at all. Two card tables pushed together against a wall and covered with a tablecloth, an Indian print bedspread, or a length of lamé can serve as a buffet. Everything on the menu must be "fork food." The stew, ragout or casserole is the mainstay of the buffet dinner—things that adhere well to a fork and do not need a knife for cutting.

Buffet dinners also solve the problem of whom to seat next to whom—"placecard blues" disappear. Let people find each other. You have other fish to fry.

Buffet meals tend to be more informal than seated dinners. If you have enough china and silver, eighteen can be served as easily as eight. A duplication of main dishes will speed up the serving line. Often the first course can be served with predinner drinks—indeed, I have planned it this way—and the salad can go along on the same plate as the entrée.

As hostess at a buffet dinner you can move from group to group. As plates start to empty you can make the rounds with the casserole or serving dish for people to help themselves to seconds. There is a sort of rhythm to parties, and buffets seem to flow smoothly without interruption. Have your husband or a male guest pour the wine. Keep an eye on debris (ashtrays and empty glasses mostly), and see that all the used dinner plates are taken out to the kitchen before dessert appears.

Food on a buffet table should be placed in order of serving: the main dish and its accompaniments first, salad next, and dessert comes later. Plates, napkins and silver should be close to the entrance of the dining room, or on the buffet table before guests reach the actual food.

The Malayan Curry Buffet dinner (page 118) is a tantalizing spread and always fun for guests to eat, especially when calories have been cut down.

105

January Jamboree Buffet for Eight

Pâté Maison
Beef Carbonnades à la Flamande
New Potatoes
Caraway Coleslaw
Lemon Chiffon Bavarian

This menu doubles nicely for sixteen guests, if you have room for them. I like to serve this kind of food in January, after the holiday parties are over. It's simple, sort of peasant-type food, with a tart dessert.

Pâté Maison

Your friends will love this pâté—homemade in your own maison.

2   tablespoons butter
2   pounds chicken livers
1   small onion, sliced
1   pound fresh mushrooms, sliced
½ cup sherry
1   teaspoon salt
½ teaspoon freshly ground black
      pepper
1   box Melba toast rounds

Melt butter in Teflon-lined pan and sauté chicken livers, sliced onions and mushrooms until livers are lightly browned and the onions and mushrooms are soft (about 15 minutes).

Place sherry, salt and pepper in blender. Add sautéed chicken-liver mixture and blend at high speed 2 minutes, until smooth. Mound on a pretty dish, or place in a crock.

Serve spread on Melba toast rounds, along with the cocktails.

Serves 8.

Beef Carbonnades à la Flamande

Once you have tasted this celebrated Belgian dish you will know why its fame persists. This is even better if made the day before.

3   pounds boneless beef chuck, cut
        in 1-inch cubes
Salt and freshly ground black
        pepper
¼   cup flour
¼   cup corn oil
9   medium onions, sliced
2   cloves garlic, pressed
2½ cups beer, any kind
2   tablespoons parsley, finely
        chopped
2   bay leaves
½   teaspoon dried thyme

Cut the beef into cubes and season well with salt and pepper. Dust meat with flour and shake off excess.

Heat the corn oil in a large Teflon skillet, add the onions and garlic, and sauté until limp and golden, but not brown. Remove and put into heavy Dutch oven.

Raise the flame, add meat to the same Teflon skillet, and brown on all sides. Do this in batches until all meat is browned. Add beer, parsley, bay leaves and thyme and cook for a minute or two, stirring to deglaze all the good brown bits from the bottom of the skillet.

Turn browned meat and skillet juices into the Dutch oven, mixing well with the onions. Cover tightly and cook over low heat 2 hours or more, until the meat is tender. This may be done the day before. Keep overnight in refrigerator and remove all congealed fat from the top before reheating.

Serve in a pretty heatproof casserole and keep hot over a candle flame or on an electric hot tray.

Serves 8.

New Potatoes

What is a low-calorie menu doing with potatoes? Contrary to most opinion, potatoes are not fattening in themselves. They are also chock-a-block full of vitamins. It is the stuff that is put on potatoes that causes the trouble—butter, gravy, sour cream. One medium-size potato contains only about 85 calories, and the two little new potatoes per person in this recipe have less than that. I dearly love potatoes and willingly give up dessert to eat one.

2 pounds of little red potatoes
        (or 2 or 3 small potatoes per
        person)
Chopped parsley

Scrub red potatoes, but do not peel. Put into a kettle with boiling salted water to cover and boil 15 to 20 minutes. Drain and quickly slip the peels off the hot potatoes (spearing them on a fork makes it easier).

Serve the potatoes *plain* in a small casserole. Sprinkle finely chopped parsley on top, and keep hot over a candle warmer or on an electric hot tray.

Serves 8.

Caraway Coleslaw

I always visualize my son-in-law making this—sleeves rolled up, digging into that pile of cabbage with his bare hands, mixing everything to a fare-thee-well. He makes the *best* coleslaw!

1 large head cabbage
1 small onion, finely chopped
½ teaspoon salt
¼ teaspoon freshly ground black
    pepper
1 tablespoon caraway seeds
Juice of 1 lemon
1 recipe Calorie-reduced
    Mayonnaise (page 187)

Shred cabbage, or cut fine with a knife. Put into a mixing bowl and sprinkle with chopped onion, salt, pepper and caraway seeds. Add lemon juice and mayonnaise and mix very well. (My son-in-law's way is really the best.)

Serves 8.

Lemon Chiffon Bavarian

Did you say diet? Nevertheless, everything that can be calorie-reduced is—and I bet you'd be surprised at the relatively low calorie count per serving.

1 cup graham cracker crumbs
2 tablespoons softened calorie-
    reduced margarine
½ teaspoon cinnamon
4 eggs, separated
Juice of 2 lemons
Grated rind of 1 lemon
½ cup sugar
1 envelope unflavored gelatin
¼ cup cold water
¼ cup hot water
1 cup calorie-reduced nondairy
    whipped topping
¼ cup crushed vanilla wafers

First make the crust. Mix together crumbs, margarine and cinnamon. Press firmly against the bottom and sides of an 8-inch spring-form pan. Chill until needed.

For the filling, beat egg yolks until thick and pale. Add lemon juice, grated lemon rind and ¼ cup of the sugar. Sprinkle gelatin in ¼ cup cold water and let soften. Then stir into ¼ cup hot water until dissolved.

Combine the egg-lemon mixture with the dissolved gelatin in the top of a double boiler and cook over hot (not boiling) water, stirring constantly until thick. Then place in refrigerator until slightly congealed.

Beat egg whites until foamy and beginning to stiffen. Add the remaining ¼ cup sugar, a teaspoonful at a time, beating until stiff and glossy. Gently fold into the lemon-gelatin mixture, then fold in whipped topping.

Pour into spring-form pan over crust, and sprinkle top with the crushed vanilla wafers. Place in refrigerator to set. Before serving, remove spring rim of pan and place dessert on cake plate.

Serves 8.

Sort of Chinese Dinner for Six

Tomato Bouillon
Hong Kong Beef
Oriental Rice
Cauliflower Salad
Brandied Pears

This comes under the heading of what to serve when you have three small steaks, and several extra people appear shortly before dinner. I visualize this as a winter meal because we are frequently snowbound, but I cooked it originally on a hot summer night when we stayed swimming until after the markets closed.

Tomato Bouillon

Prepare this early in the day and chill in the refrigerator if the weather is warm. If you are really pushed, and it's the last minute, pour over rocks (ice cubes) in old-fashioned glasses.

4 cups tomato juice
1 cup boiling water
3 teaspoons beef extract (or 2 beef bouillon cubes)
1 tablespoon grated onion
¼ teaspoon celery seed

Combine all ingredients and bring to a boil. Serve in mugs.
Serves 6.

Hong Kong Beef

2 tablespoons corn oil
8 scallions and stems, chopped
2 cloves garlic, pressed
5 stalks celery, sliced on bias
1 tablespoon (or more) soy sauce, to taste
3 boneless club steaks, cut in 1-inch strips, all fat removed
1 large green pepper, cut in 1-inch squares
16-ounce can bean sprouts, rinsed and drained
5-ounce can bamboo shoots
16-ounce can fancy Chinese vegetables
½ pound fresh mushrooms, sliced through stems (or 4¼-ounce can sliced mushrooms)
9-ounce package frozen snow peas, just thawed
2 cups Fat-free Beef Bouillon (page 192 or 193)
3 tablespoons cornstarch
⅓ cup cold water

Heat oil in a very large skillet (or a Chinese wok), add scallions, garlic and celery, and sauté 5 minutes. Add 1 tablespoon soy sauce, or more, to taste.

Add beef and remaining vegetables except snow peas. Cook over high heat, uncovered, stirring constantly, 5 minutes. Add thawed snow peas. Keep turning with a wide spatula over high heat for 2 minutes more. Add hot bouillon and lower the flame to simmer.

Mix cornstarch with the cold water. Slowly stir into the sauce and keep stirring until sauce is transparent and thickens enough to coat spoon. Taste for seasoning and add more soy sauce if needed. Serve at once.

Serves 6.

Oriental Rice

Rice has the reputation of being fattening. But how many fat Chinese and Japanese are there? And what are they feeding all those fatties down at Duke University who are trying to lose weight? Rice! But with a difference. They have pared away the other calories. Half a cup of cooked rice contains 100 calories. Can you afford it? If you are exceeding your caloric budget, skip the rice and eat the Hong Kong Beef without it. Orientals like rice that is slightly sticky—easier to eat with chopsticks, of course.

1½ cups long grain rice
1 teaspoon salt
3 cups water

Thoroughly wash rice in several changes of cold water. Bring 3 cups salted water to a boil in a heavy saucepan, Teflon if possible. Add washed rice. Stir well, and cover.

Reduce heat to lowest, and cook very slowly 25 minutes. All the water will be absorbed and the rice should be moist and tender.

Put into a deep, hot serving dish and keep hot over a candle warmer or on an electric hot tray.

Serves 6.

Cauliflower Salad

This is a great way to stretch a little cauliflower (or one frozen package) to feed extra guests.

1 small cauliflower (or 10-ounce frozen package)
½ teaspoon sugar
½ teaspoon salt
¼ teaspoon pepper
2 teaspoons grated lemon rind
2 tablespoons lemon juice
2 tablespoons onion, finely chopped
1 clove garlic, pressed
4 tablespoons olive oil
1 small head iceberg lettuce
¼ green pepper, cut in strips
½ 3-ounce jar pimiento, drained and sliced
¼ teaspoon freshly ground black pepper
4 hard-cooked eggs, quartered

Put cauliflower into lots of boiling salted water, cover, and boil until tender but still crisp—6 to 8 minutes. (Cook frozen cauliflower according to package directions.) Drain and separate into flowerets as soon as it is cool enough to handle. Put into a bowl (not metal), and reserve.

Make a marinade of sugar, salt, pepper, grated lemon rind, lemon juice, onion, garlic and oil. Pour over cauliflower while still warm. Let sit for 30 minutes or more. Cover with plastic wrap and put into refrigerator to chill.

Hard-boil eggs. When cool enough to handle, shell and cut into quarters. Reserve.

Drain the cauliflower, reserving the marinade. Line your salad bowl with lettuce leaves. Add cauliflower, green pepper and pimiento. Pour reserved marinade over the salad. Toss lightly. Place quartered hard-cooked eggs around the edge and grind black pepper over all. Serve at once. Serves 6.

Brandied Pears

These can be served hot or cold, depending on how much notice you have of this little gathering and what the weather is at the moment. If you don't have canned pears on your emergency shelf, use peaches or even apricots.

2 16-ounce cans calorie-reduced pear halves
½ cup calorie-reduced strawberry preserves
¼ cup peach or apricot brandy

Simmer pears in their own juice 10 minutes, uncovered. Stir in preserves and brandy. Continue to simmer 10 minutes. Serve in individual dessert dishes with a little of the sauce spooned over each serving. Serves 6.

Country Captain Dinner for Six

Honeydew Nova Scotia
Country Captain Chicken
Vegetables à la Grecque
Macédoine of Fruits en Gelée

The joy of this menu is that everything is done ahead of time, and all you have to do is the pleasant job of arranging the flowers and a little light dusting. Country Captain is a favorite among regular army people—it makes a little chicken go a long, long, way, a genuine help in these days of the sky-rocketing budget.

Honeydew Nova Scotia

This is easy to eat at a buffet because you have removed the melon rind, and it cuts easily with a fork.

1   small ripe honeydew melon
Curly chicory
½ pound Nova Scotia smoked
  salmon
Freshly ground black pepper
Lemon wedges, for garnish

Chill melon thoroughly and cut into slender slices. They look like little new moons. Remove rind.

Place on a bed of curly chicory, alternating slices of melon with slices of smoked salmon.

Grind black pepper over the melon and salmon to bring out the flavor of both. Garnish with lemon wedges.

Serves 6.

Country Captain Chicken

The combination of spices in this recipe gives a new taste to chicken. And what an aroma!

2   2½-pound chickens, disjointed
1   teaspoon salt
¼   teaspoon pepper
½   cup flour
¼   cup salad oil
1   teaspoon seasoned salt
2   onions, finely chopped
1   clove garlic, pressed
2   green peppers, finely chopped
¼   cup parsley, finely chopped
16-ounce can tomatoes
1   teaspoon mace
1   teaspoon curry
¼   teaspoon paprika
½   cup dried currants (or raisins)
½   cup toasted, slivered almonds

Rub the chicken with salt and pepper. Put the flour in a paper bag and shake well with a few pieces of chicken at a time.

Heat oil in a large Teflon skillet, add chicken pieces, sprinkle with seasoned salt, and brown well. You may have to do this in several batches in order not to crowd chicken. Remove chicken as it browns to a large casserole.

In the same Teflon skillet brown onions, garlic, green pepper and parsley. Add tomatoes and season with mace, curry and paprika. Simmer sauce 15 minutes, then pour over chicken in casserole.

Cover casserole tightly and place in a preheated 300° oven 1½ hours, or until chicken is literally falling off the bones. Sprinkle with currants (or raisins), cook 5 minutes more, sprinkle with slivered almonds, and serve at once.

Serves 6.

Vegetables à la Grecque

The lettuce cups keep the salad nicely separated from the other food on the dinner plates, eliminating the need for salad plates.

2   10-ounce packages frozen mixed
      vegetables
1   recipe Oil and Vinegar Dressing
      (page 189)
1   clove garlic, pressed
2   tablespoons Parmesan cheese,
      freshly grated
½   cup celery (1 8-inch stalk),
      finely diced
½   green pepper, finely chopped
6   cupped lettuce leaves

Cook the vegetables according to

package directions. Make the Oil and Vinegar Dressing and add garlic and Parmesan to it.

Drain mixed vegetables and put into a bowl (not metal). Add celery and green pepper, then pour the dressing over the warm vegetables. Cover and chill in the refrigerator until serving time.

Divide vegetable mixture among 6 lettuce cups and place them on an oval serving platter.

Serves 6.

Macédoine of Fruits en Gelée

8-ounce can unsweetened
    pineapple tidbits
16-ounce can calorie-reduced
    sliced peaches
8-ounce can calorie-reduced
    mandarin oranges
2   envelopes unflavored gelatin
1¼ cups unsweetened grapefruit
    juice
½   cup rosé wine
Few drops red food coloring
    (optional)
1   cup seedless white grapes
2   fresh pears, pared, cored and
    diced

Drain pineapple, peaches and mandarin oranges, reserving juices.

Set fruit aside. Sprinkle gelatin over reserved fruit juices and let soften.

Bring grapefruit juice to a boil. Add softened gelatin and stir well until it dissolves. Stir in wine (and food coloring if desired).

Refrigerate gelatin mixture until it begins to thicken, about 45 minutes to an hour. Place reserved fruits in layers in a crystal bowl—oranges, grapes, pineapple, peaches and pears, in that order. Carefully pour the slightly thickened gelatin over fruit. Refrigerate until set.

At serving time place crystal bowl on a silver tray, and serve directly from bowl to dessert dishes.

Serves 6.

All Seasons Buffet for Six

Colorful Cabbage Bowl
Tongue Creole
Creamed Spinach
Escarole à l'Indienne
Grape Mold Royale

This is one of my favorite menus. I love tongue, especially when it is covered with Creole sauce. It's delicious, and available the year round—and it makes a lovely party.

Colorful Cabbage Bowl

1 recipe **Zesty Dip** (page 190)
1 large head cabbage
3 carrots
1 cauliflower
1 bunch radishes
1 cucumber
2 green peppers
1 bunch scallions

Make Zesty Dip the day before, so flavors blend. Keep covered in refrigerator until needed. With a sharp paring knife, hollow out center of cabbage. Leave a rim about 1 inch wide. (Save the inside of the cabbage for coleslaw.) Cut a slice off the stem end so the cabbage will sit evenly. Curl the outer leaves of the cabbage down toward the outside so it looks like a big flower.

Cut carrot sticks, cauliflowerets, radish roses, cucumber sticks, and green pepper sticks, and trim scallions. You can do these early in the day and keep in bowls of ice water in the refrigerator. Drain and pat dry before arranging around cabbage.

To serve, fill center of cabbage with Zesty Dip and set on a large tray. Surround with the crisp vegetables arranged in pretty groups of contrasting colors.

Serves 6.

Tongue Creole

The tongue should be so tender that it is easily cut with a fork.

4- to 5-pound tongue, fresh, pickled or smoked
2   medium onions, chopped
3   whole stalks celery, with leaves
1   bay leaf
1   teaspoon pickling spice
1   garlic clove
1   tablespoon butter

1   large onion, diced
1   green pepper, diced
2   stalks celery, diced
1   pound fresh mushrooms, sliced (or 2 8-ounce cans)
1½ cups tomato sauce
1   cup defatted tongue stock

Place tongue, chopped onions, whole celery stalks, bay leaf, pickling spice and garlic in a large kettle, cover with water and bring to a boil. Reduce heat and simmer slowly for about 3 hours, or until tongue is fork tender. Lift out tongue, skin, and trim base while still warm. Return tongue to pot and keep warm.

Draw off a cupful of the stock, chill, and remove the layer of fat that congeals on top. Reserve this defatted stock for the sauce.

To make the Creole sauce, heat 1 tablespoon butter in a Teflon pan and sauté onion, green pepper, celery and mushrooms until onion is limp and mushrooms give up their liquor (about 12 minutes). Add tomato sauce and the reserved defatted tongue stock. Blend thoroughly. Let simmer, uncovered, until it is reduced to the right consistency—it should be about as thick as catsup.

I like to serve this in a chafing dish. Slice tongue in diagonal slices, place in a chafing dish over a low, warming flame, and carefully cover with sauce.

Serves 6.

Creamed Spinach

Spinach traditionally is served with tongue; the reason escapes me, except that they do go well together.

3 10-ounce packages frozen
   chopped spinach
3 tablespoons chopped chives
Juice of 1 lemon
¼ cup plain yogurt
¼ teaspoon nutmeg
½ teaspoon salt
¼ teaspoon freshly ground black
   pepper

Cook spinach according to package directions. Drain very well.

Mix all the other ingredients. Place one-third of this mixture in the blender with one-third of the spinach and blend 15 seconds at high speed. Repeat in two more batches until all blended. Combine all in heated serving dish and serve.

Serves 6.

Escarole à l'Indienne

While your taste buds are still reeling from the Creole sauce, this provides something tangy enough to make an impression.

1 recipe Oil and Vinegar Salad
   Dressing (page 189)
½ teaspoon curry powder
½ teaspoon grated onion
1 large head escarole

Make dressing. Add curry powder and onion and mix well, or shake in a bottle.

Wash and dry the escarole. Wrap *each* piece in paper towel and roll up. Place in vegetable crisper.

When ready to make salad, tear escarole into bite-size pieces and put into salad bowl. Shake dressing again, then pour over escarole, toss well, and serve at once.

Serves 6.

Grape Mold Royale

1½ envelopes unflavored gelatin
¼   cup cold water
2   teaspoons grated orange rind
2   teaspoons grated lemon rind
¼   teaspoon salt
½   cup sugar
1   cup boiling water
½   cup orange juice
¼   cup lemon juice
5   eggs, separated
1   teaspoon vanilla extract
2   cups seedless white grapes
Grape clusters and orange slices for garnish (optional)

Sprinkle gelatin over ¼ cup cold water and let stand 5 minutes to soften. In top of double boiler over hot (not boiling) water, combine softened gelatin, orange rind, lemon rind, salt and sugar. Gradually add boiling water, orange juice, lemon juice, and well-beaten egg yolks. Continue to cook over hot (not boiling) water, stirring constantly, until mixture thickens (about 12 to 15 minutes). Remove from heat. Stir in vanilla.

Chill until mixture begins to mound when dropped from a spoon. Beat egg whites until stiff peaks form. Fold into chilled gelatin mixture. Spoon into a lightly oiled 6-cup mold, adding the grapes as you do so. Chill until firm.

To unmold, carefully run a small sharp knife around the edges of the mold. Turn mold upside down on a chilled serving dish. Wring out a clean dish towel in very hot water and place closely over the mold for about a minute. (The heat of the towel will soften the gelatin just a little.) Grasping mold and plate together firmly, give a sharp little shake, and gelatin will slip out of the mold onto the plate. Lift off the mold.

Garnish serving plate with little clusters of white grapes and orange sections if desired.

Serves 6.

Malayan Curry Buffet for Eight

Malayan Curry
Saffron Rice
Dal (Lentil Purée)
Accompaniments:
Chopped Tomatoes
Chopped Hard-cooked Eggs
Chopped Parsley, Mango Chunks
Coconut, Cucumber Chunks
Hot Sauce, Yogurt, and
Maddy's Green Apple Chutney
Assorted Melons

This is probably the most complicated menu in the book. The time to make the green apple chutney is when apples are green in August. The Dal must be made the day before the party. There is a great deal of chopping, mincing and grating, so I plan this meal when one of my "cooking friends"

comes to visit. Children old enough to be entrusted with a knife can also be enlisted to help.

Malayan Curry

4 pounds boneless lamb (leg or shoulder)
2 tablespoons corn oil
2 onions, chopped
4 cloves garlic, pressed
Salt and pepper
1½ teaspoons curry powder
2 teaspoons flour
1¼ teaspoons powdered ginger
1 tablespoon cinnamon
1¼ teaspoons turmeric
2 tablespoons pounded coriander
1 tablespoon, or less, to taste, crushed and powdered chili peppers (hot, hot!)
1 tablespoon chopped fresh lemon balm or thyme (optional)
2 cups Fat-free Chicken Bouillon (page 192 or 193)

Cut raw lamb into 1-inch chunks, trimming off all fat. Heat oil in a large Teflon pan and put in onions, garlic and meat, and salt and pepper to taste. Cook, stirring occasionally, 10 minutes, until everything begins to take on color. Do not allow to brown. Take off the heat and set on the back of the stove to keep warm.

Put curry powder, flour, ginger, cinnamon, turmeric, coriander, lemon balm (or thyme) and chili pepper into a bowl. Slowly dribble in a little of the hot chicken bouillon, stirring, until it makes a smooth paste. Smoothly stir in the rest of the chicken bouillon.

Add curry mixture to the lamb in the Teflon pan, mixing well. Put over a high flame until it begins to bubble; at once lower the flame, cover tightly, and simmer 1 to 1½ hours, until very tender.

Serve in a casserole over a candle warmer or an electric hot tray.

Serves 8.

Saffron Rice

The same story goes for this rice as the rice on page 110—100 calories for one-half cup.

4 cups water
1 tablespoon salt
2 cups long grain rice
¼ teaspoon powdered saffron

Bring 4 cups salted water to a boil and add rice. Lower flame, cover tightly and simmer very slowly. After 5 minutes, stir in the saffron with a fork. Continue slowly simmering the rice until tender and the liquid is absorbed, about 20 minutes more.

Serve in an open casserole and keep warm over a candle warmer or on an electric hot tray.

Serves 8.

Dal (*Lentil Purée*)

This is the classic Indian accompaniment to a curry, and you can see why —it's both bland and very tasty. Make this the night before. You no longer have to soak lentils overnight, but I still do it.

1   cup dried lentils
1   large onion, sliced
2   tablespoons butter
2½ cups Fat-free Chicken Bouillon
       (page 192 or 193)
Salt and pepper to taste

Soak lentils overnight. Drain. Slice onion thin. Melt 2 tablespoons butter in a Teflon pan and sauté onion until it is golden.

Remove pan from heat and pour in boiling stock. Add lentils and salt and pepper to taste. Bring to a boil, then reduce heat and simmer, covered, until lentils are tender, about half an hour. Stir often with a wooden spoon to keep the lentils from sticking.

When the lentils are done they will have absorbed all the liquid and your stirring will have broken them down to a rough purée. Serve hot.

Serves 8.

Maddy's Green Apple Chutney

This chutney is called Maddy's because she is the one who gives me the green apples from her tree in August. If you like it less peppery, just reduce (or leave out) the red peppers; it will be just as delicious.

10 cups green apples, peeled, cored,
      and diced
4   cups vinegar
2   lemons, seeded and diced
15-ounce box seedless raisins
6   ounces crystalized ginger
2   cups calorie-reduced maple
      syrup
1   tablespoon salt
½   teaspoon cayenne pepper
3   small hot red peppers (or less,
      to taste), minced

16-ounce package frozen chopped
    onions
2-ounce jar mustard seeds

Combine all ingredients in stainless kettle (steel or enamel) and cook over medium low heat, covered, 3½ hours. Stir frequently. Pack into sterilized jars and seal. Let age 2 or 3 weeks before using.

Makes 5½ pints.

Curry Accompaniments

As we have nine accompaniments, I guess we could call this a nine-boy curry. Where you could rustle up nine boys at short notice I really don't know, unless you are running a summer camp or are a den mother.

Tomatoes:
>   4 ripe tomatoes, skinned,
>   seeded, and chopped

Hard-cooked eggs:
>   4 eggs, chopped

Parsley:
>   1 cup, finely chopped

Cucumber:
>   2 cucumbers, peeled and cut in
>   chunks

Coconut:
>   1 fresh coconut, grated

Mangoes:
>   2 fresh (or 1-pound 4-ounce
>   can, rinsed and drained),
>   cut in chunks

Yogurt:
>   2 containers, plain *ice* cold

Bottled hot sauce:
>   (sometimes called
>   Louisiana sauce)

Maddy's Green Apple Chutney
>   (page 120)

Put accompaniments in individual bowls in the center of table or on a lazy Susan, surrounding the curry, the rice, and the Dal.

Serves 8.

Assorted Melons

This is wonderful for cooling off after that hot curry. The assortment depends on the melons you find in your market. If all else fails you can usually find frozen melon balls in your grocer's freezer.

1 honeydew
1 cantaloupe
1 Persian
1 Cranshaw
¼ watermelon
>   or
4 10-ounce packages frozen melon
>   balls, just thawed

I like to make crescent-shaped slices of honeydew, cantaloupe, Persian, Cranshaw or watermelon. Peel the slices so they are easy to eat with a fork.

Serve icy cold on a large silver platter, arranged in contrasting colors in circles.

Serves 8.

Continental Dinner for Six

Savory Eggs
Marjorie's Escalope de Veau
Carrot Ring with Fresh Peas
Mushroom Salad
Soufflé Citron

With its Escalope de Veau and Soufflé Citron, this is a lovely menu in the French style. And it's another one good any time of year—not too hot and steamy for July, not too cool for February.

Savory Eggs

6   hard-cooked eggs
3¾-ounce can skinless and boneless sardines, packed with no added oil
2   tablespoons Calorie-reduced Mayonnaise (page 187)

2   teaspoons chopped sweet gherkins
Salt and pepper
Watercress (or parsley) sprigs, for garnish

Hard-boil eggs, shell, and cut in half lengthwise. Trim a very thin slice off the bottom of each half so eggs will sit firmly and not slide around. Gently scoop out yolks.

Using a fork, mash yolks with sardines. Add mayonnaise and mix until smooth. Stir in chopped sweet gherkins. Salt and pepper to taste.

Mound this mixture into the egg whites and serve, garnished with watercress (or parsley) sprigs.

Serves 6.

Marjorie's Escalope de Veau

This delicious dish can be made in a chafing dish at the table, or conventionally, in the kitchen.

1 tablespoon butter
1 tablespoon flour
1 cup Fat-free Beef Bouillon
    (page 192 or 193)
1 tablespoon Worcestershire sauce
2 pounds veal scallops, thinly sliced
2 tablespoons olive oil
2 cloves garlic, pressed
2 medium onions, sliced
2 green peppers, chopped
3 large tomatoes, skinned, seeded,
    and diced (or 1 pound canned
    tomatoes, drained)
Salt and pepper to taste

First make a brown sauce: melt butter in small sauce pan. Stir in flour with a wire whisk and brown well. Stir in beef bouillon and Worcestershire sauce and bring to a boil. This can be done ahead of time. Reserve on back of stove until needed, then quickly reheat.

Pat veal scallops dry with paper towels. Heat oil in a large—preferably Teflon—skillet, add garlic, onions, and green pepper, and sauté until limp. Push to one side. Add veal scallops to the skillet a few at a time, turn the heat up high, and sauté the meat until brown. Add the tomatoes and season with salt and pepper to taste. Stir in the reserved (hot) brown sauce, simmer for a few minutes, and serve at once.

Serves 6.

Carrot Ring with Fresh Peas

Surprisingly nicer than the usual mixed carrots and peas.

3 1-pound bunches tender young
    carrots
3 tablespoons butter
3 egg yolks
2 tablespoons chopped chives
Pinch of ground cloves
Pepper to taste
2 pounds fresh peas, shelled (or 3
    9-ounce packages frozen peas
    cooked with 1 medium-size
    onion)

Cook carrots in boiling salted water until very tender. Drain and divide into 3 batches. Place each batch in blender with 1 egg yolk and 1 tablespoon melted butter per batch. Add chives, cloves, and pepper to the last batch. As each batch is blended smooth, turn it into a large bowl and mix all very well. Turn into a lightly oiled 6-cup ring mold.

Place ring mold in a pan of hot water in a preheated 350° oven and bake 35 minutes. Unmold (as directed on page 39) onto a hot serving plate.

While ring mold is cooking, shell fresh peas and cook in lightly salted boiling water until just tender. (Or cook frozen peas according to package directions, adding one peeled medium size onion. Discard onion.) Drain peas and keep hot until needed.

Fill center of carrot ring with hot green peas. Keep warm on an electric hot tray.

Serves 6.

Mushroom Salad

1 recipe Oil and Lemon Dressing (page 189)
18 large mushrooms, sliced
4 7-inch celery stalks, finely minced
2 medium onions, finely minced
4-ounce can sliced pimientos
¼ cup black olives, pitted and sliced
6 cupped lettuce leaves

Make Oil and Lemon Dressing and set aside. Mix the remaining ingredients (except lettuce) in a large bowl. Shake dressing, pour over all, and toss well.

Set cupped lettuce leaves on a pretty serving dish and fill with individual servings of the mushroom salad.

Serves 6.

Soufflé Citron

1 envelope unflavored gelatin
¼ cup cold water
1 teaspoon grated lemon rind
Juice of approximately 3 lemons (to make ½ cup)
4 eggs, separated
½ cup sugar
½ teaspoon salt
1 cup calorie-reduced nondairy whipped topping

Tie a waxed paper collar around the top of a 1-quart soufflé dish, allowing the paper to rise about 4 inches above the rim. Chill the dish.

Sprinkle gelatin over cold water and put aside to soften.

Grate enough lemon rind to measure 1 teaspoon. Squeeze the lemons to make ½ cup of juice. Separate eggs. Put yolks into the top of a double boiler over hot (not boiling) water. Stir in lemon juice, sugar and salt. Cook over hot water, stirring constantly, until thick and custardy, about 10 minutes. Stir in softened gelatin. Add grated lemon rind. Pour into a large bowl and let cool.

Beat egg whites until they are stiff and form peaks. Pile whipped topping on top of stiff egg whites and gently fold the whole thing into the lemon mixture. Pour at once into chilled soufflé dish and chill until firm but spongy (about 2 or 3 hours). Remove paper collar and serve dessert with pride.

Serves 6.

CHAPTER SIX

Portable Parties

The best parties are often the least formal ones. This is not to say that they are less carefully planned and organized in advance. An army travels on its stomach, and a party rises or falls on the quality of the drinks, the food and the guest list.

The first warm day of spring sends us flocking to the country, picnic basket in hand. A crisp autumn Saturday inspires a lunch served from the tailgate of a station wagon before the Big Game. It is important to remember calories when planning the menu. Along with the ants there are other traditional aspects to picnics, and I wouldn't dream of changing them. I am merely adjusting some of the ingredients to suit our weight-watching needs.

Sometimes the food needs only to be toted across your own garden to poolside, or to the terrace beside the barbecue. Perhaps in the fall you will serve a Sunday afternoon "between the halves" picnic in front of a roaring fire, for the pro football fans who surely inhabit nearly every house in the land. Consider the growing army, or should I say navy, of boat owners. Any mate would rather be up on deck than trapped slaving in the galley below. Preplanning makes this possible.

Traffic being what it is today (monstrous), many hostesses are hiring buses to transport their guests to balls, exhibitions, and sports events. I attended a "moving experience" last year in Chicago. All the out-of-town guests at a large wedding were picked up at their hotels in a bus, complete with tour director, driver, bride, groom and wedding attendants, and two white-coated butlers who served drinks and delicious homemade picnic fare

Tailgate Picnic for Six (page 135) is a complete
outdoor feast—reduced in calories, portable and
hearty enough for the most active appetites.

as we were driven about the city. The tour stopped at the Museum of Science and Industry and the only hitch to the whole affair was trying to wrench the group away from that fascinating place.

There is no need for anyone to give up all the fun and games that accompany a moveable feast. All you need is a little help and advice from the lady with the leastest—calories, that is.

Here are the secrets of successful picnics. It's the equipment, gear and accessories that make it easy to assemble and cart your food to whatever bucolic spot you wish to visit, be it far or near. Take enough of everything, but remember you are not going to a desert island.

Essential List of Picnic Gear

Tablecloth (paper tablecloths fly away in the wind, and plastic doesn't settle nicely onto the turf. You can find beautiful tablecloths nowadays that drip dry and don't even need the touch of an iron)

Napkins (heavy paper will do, but I use terry cloth ones)

Bottle opener-cum-corkscrew

Fruit knife

Paring knife

Carving knife

Salt and pepper

Paper towels

Forks and spoons (*not* plastic)

Glasses (thin plastic ones are good)

Insect repellent

Plastic bags for refuse (please carry away)

First-aid kit

Picnic baskets and carriers: insulated bags, plastic cooler boxes, and "canned ice" (various shapes, sizes and brands of "canned ice" are available—you freeze the cans, and pack in your insulated container with the food you wish to keep cold. This "dry ice" can be used over and over, and eliminates messy melting and dripping).

Packets of disposable waterless towelettes for hand washing

Thermos jugs for coffee, tea, lemonade, and just plain water

The big deal in picnics (as in almost everything) is advance preparation. The fire that won't burn, the dessert that dissolves, the main dish left home in the refrigerator are disasters you can avoid by planning ahead, making lists, and remembering to check them.

First, make the guest list. Don't ask people who hate the outdoors. Don't overcrowd your vehicle. Plan your destination. Plan your menu. Make your marketing list. I do my shopping early in the week when stores are uncrowded. I prepare as much of the food as possible the day before. Pray for a nice day. Have a beautiful picnic!

Picnic in the Park for Six

Crab-stuffed Tomatoes
Crunchy Chicken Legs
Picnic Salad
Fresh Peaches

This is a great picnic to take along for a late-summer day in the park. The only thing I would add to it is iced dry white wine—and I'd pack a little wicker hamper with my good wine glasses, too.

Crab-stuffed Tomatoes

Don't forget your fish forks!

6 **medium tomatoes**
½ **recipe Calorie-reduced Mayonnaise** (page 187)
¼ **cup green onions, finely chopped**
1 **tablespoon chopped chives**
1 **teaspoon dried tarragon**
1 **tablespoon chopped parsley**
1 **tablespoon sweet basil** (or ½ teaspoon dried)
2 **cloves garlic, pressed**
½ **pound crab meat** (fresh, frozen or canned), **picked over**
Salt and pepper to taste

Cut the tops off the tomatoes and reserve. Scoop the insides out of the tomatoes and turn upside down to drain.

Make the mayonnaise, combine it with the remaining ingredients, and mix well. Fill the tomatoes with the crab mixture and put the tomato hats back on.

Arrange in a shallow dish that will fit in your cooler bag. Cover with plastic wrap and keep refrigerated until ready to transport to the picnic.

Serves 6.

Crunchy Chicken Legs

1 tablespoon prepared mustard
½ 13-ounce can evaporated skim
   milk
12 drumsticks
Salt and pepper to taste
1 cup crushed cornflakes

Mix the mustard with the evaporated milk in a bowl. Season the chicken legs with salt and pepper. Dip the legs in the mustard-milk mixture. Lift out and let them drip a minute, then roll them in the crushed cornflakes.

Put them on a Teflon cookie sheet and bake in a preheated 375° oven 50 minutes, turning them once. They will be crisp and golden.

Serve hot, tepid, or cool with paper napkins to hold.

Serves 6.

Picnic Salad

I have a lazy Susan that travels well; the Susan part is made of tortoise plastic and the dishes that fit in it stack well.

1 recipe Sour Cream Dip
   (page 190)
1-pound bag red radishes
½-pound bag white radishes
½ pound small carrots, cut into
   sticks
1 bunch celery, cut into sticks
4 zucchini, about 6 inches long, cut
   into sticks
1 cauliflower, broken into flowerets

Make Sour Cream Dip and clean and prepare vegetables. Put vegetables in plastic bags and keep in refrigerator until time to serve.

At picnic time, put the dip into a wide-mouthed Thermos jug for toting. Transfer the vegetables in their plastic bags straight from refrigerator to cooler bag.

Serves 6.

Fresh Peaches

My husband has been known to cut up his peach and dunk the pieces in his glass of white wine. Don't knock it till you've tried it.

12 peaches (more if they are small)

Transport chilled peaches to picnic in plastic bags. If there is room for them in your cooler bag, fine; if not—they are just as good at park temperature.

Serves 6.

Poolside Sunday Supper for Eight

London Broil
Green Beans Vinaigrette
Tomatoes and Red Onion Rings
Petits Pots de Chocolat

How heavenly it is to get all the work done the day before the party! This is especially nice if you have house guests, because you can enjoy being with them instead of being locked to the stove, missing all the fun.

London Broil

4-pound London Broil, 2 inches thick
Salt and pepper
2 teaspoons Worcestershire sauce
1 medium onion, grated
1 clove garlic, pressed
1 tablespoon lemon juice
1 small green pepper, seeded and
    sliced into rings

Rub steak with everything but the green pepper rings and marinate for several hours with the green peppers strewn on top. If marinated in the morning, keep meat at room temperature until ready to cook. If done the day before, refrigerate until 3 hours before serving time; then keep at room temperature.

Drain steak and transfer to the preheated broiler pan and place 3 inches below the flame. Broil to the desired degree of rareness, turning once (12 minutes to a side for rare; 15 for medium rare; 17 for medium well; 20 for well done). Put on a wooden board, slice thinly on the bias, and carry out to poolside.

Serves 8.

Green Beans Vinaigrette

If you have unaccountably run out of greens for salad, don't drop everything and rush to the store. Just reach in the freezer for some French-style green beans and proceed as follows.

1   recipe Oil and Vinegar Dressing
      (page 189)
4   10-ounce packages frozen
      French-style green beans
¼ cup parsley, finely chopped

Make Oil and Vinegar Dressing. Cook beans according to package directions. Drain. Put beans in a bowl (not metal) while still hot, and pour dressing over them. Cover and place in refrigerator to chill.

At serving time, place dressed green beans in serving dish and sprinkle with chopped parsley.
Serves 8.

Tomatoes and Red Onion Rings

Summertime brings us beautiful tomatoes, so let's use them almost unadorned. What could be better?

6   of the biggest, reddest tomatoes
      you can find
4   comparable-size red onions
1   tablespoon dried oregano
½ cup red wine vinegar
Freshly ground black pepper
      (optional)

Slice the tomatoes about ¼ inch thick; ditto the red onions. Alternate them in overlapping slices on a large platter. Sprinkle with oregano and drizzle the red wine vinegar over all. Pass the pepper grinder for those who will.
Serves 8.

Petits Pots de Chocolat

2-ounce package calorie-reduced
      chocolate pudding
4   cups skim milk for pudding
½ cup semisweet chocolate bits
1   cup calorie-reduced nondairy
      whipped topping
4   tablespoons light rum

Combine pudding mix, milk, and chocolate bits. Cook over medium heat until mixture comes to a boil, stirring constantly. Lower flame and continue to cook, stirring, until chocolate bits are all melted. Put into a bowl (not metal), cover, and place in refrigerator until chilled. Beat smooth with an electric beater. Fold in the whipped topping and rum. Spoon into little chocolate pots. Chill until needed.
Serves 8.

Elegant Picnic for Six

Cream of Cucumber Soup
Stuffed Lobster
Asparagus en Salade
Mandarin Oranges in Lemon Shells

Come summer and the performing arts move outdoors. Summer stock, music in the round, concerts—all of them are happening under the stars. This is an elegant meal, inspired by the opera at Glyndebourne in England, where everyone picnics in formal garb.

Cream of Cucumber Soup

2 cucumbers, pared and sliced
1 onion, finely chopped
4 cups Fat-free Chicken Bouillon (page 192 or 193)
¼ teaspoon white pepper
1 bay leaf
1 tablespoon cornstarch
3 tablespoons cold water
1 teaspoon salt
1 cup skim milk
1 tablespoon fresh dill, finely chopped (or 1½ teaspoons dried dill weed)

Combine the cucumbers, onion, chicken bouillon, pepper and bay leaf in a saucepan. Bring to a boil, then simmer covered over low heat 20 minutes. Fish out the bay leaf.

Purée the soup in a food mill, or push through a sieve. Return to saucepan.

Put the cornstarch and water into a cup, mix until smooth, and stir it into the soup. Cook over low heat, stirring constantly until the soup comes just to a boil. Remove from heat. Salt to taste, add milk, and taste again. Put into a covered (not metal) bowl and chill. Also chill soup plates.

Put chilled soup in cold Thermos jug and pack in the picnic cooler along with chilled soup plates. Carry the dill in a plastic bag (or take along the bottle of dill weed). Sprinkle with dill just before serving.

Serves 6.

Stuffed Lobster

12 7-ounce lobster tails (or 6 12-
ounce tails) (available frozen)
1 tablespoon butter
2 tablespoons grated onion
¼ cup flour
1 cup Fat-free Chicken Bouillon
(page 192 or 193)
½ pound fresh mushrooms, chopped
2 cups skim milk
Juice of 1½ lemons
½ cup fine cracker crumbs
¼ cup Parmesan cheese, grated
Paprika

Cook lobster tails as directed on
the package. Drain, and when cool
enough to handle remove meat from
shells, reserving shells for stuffing
later. Cut lobster meat in small dice.

Melt butter in a Teflon pan and
sauté lobster meat and grated onion
in it 2 minutes. Stir in flour, chicken
bouillon, mushrooms and skim milk.
Cook, stirring constantly, over medium heat until mixture thickens.
Stir in lemon juice.

Spoon lobster mixture into the
lobster shells. Mix together crumbs
and Parmesan cheese and sprinkle
over lobsters. Dust with paprika.
Bake in preheated 450° oven 10 minutes. Immediately refrigerate until
time to pack in the cooler.
Serves 6.

Asparagus en Salade

1 recipe Oil and Vinegar Dressing
(page 189)
1 tablespoon sweet pepper relish
3 10-ounce packages frozen
asparagus spears

Make Oil and Vinegar Dressing
and add to it 1 tablespoon sweet
pepper relish.
Cook the asparagus spears as directed on the package. Drain thoroughly on paper towels. While still
warm, put asparagus into a rimmed
dish, cover with the dressing, and
allow to cool at room temperature.

Put into a rimmed plastic container with a tight-fitting lid, and
carry to the picnic. This is served at
room temperature.
Serves 6.

Mandarin Oranges in Lemon Shells

6 really large lemons
3 8-ounce cans calorie-reduced
mandarin oranges
6 tablespoons orange liqueur

Cut ¾-inch slice off tops of lemons
and a thin slice off bottoms (so they
will sit level) and scoop out pulp.
Drain orange sections, put into a
bowl (not metal), and mix with the
orange liqueur.

Put the lemon shells in a muffin
tin, pile in the orange mixture and
chill until time to leave for the picnic. Cover with plastic wrap, and
transport them in the muffin tin inside your cooler bag. Take little
dessert plates to put them on for
serving.
Serves 6.

Tailgate Picnic for Six

Portable Deviled Eggs
Rock Cornish Hens
Marinated Broccoli
Fruit in the Hand

When the fine weather beckons, pack the picnic basket and get an early start for the country or the beach. Your portable cooler will keep your lunch at the right temperature while you work up an appetite. You can play golf or tennis, stroll through the woodlands or just park near a convenient dune and spend a beautiful day at the beach.

Portable Deviled Eggs

6 hard-cooked eggs
6 large, fresh mushrooms
1 tablespoon finely chopped
    scallion
1 teaspoon parsley, finely chopped
1 tablespoon butter
1 tablespoon dry sherry
½ teaspoon salt
⅛ teaspoon black pepper
Paprika and parsley sprigs for
    garnish

Slice eggs in half crosswise, not the way you usually do. Remove yolks and mash them with a fork. Reserve the whites. Chop the fresh mushrooms, add chopped scallion and parsley. Melt the butter in a little Teflon-lined pan and add the mushroom mixture. Sauté until the mushrooms release their juice, then add sherry, salt and pepper. Blend mushroom mixture into the mashed egg yolks. Fill egg whites with this stuffing, mounding it up in a cone shape. Sprinkle with paprika and garnish with little parsley sprigs.

Place your 12 stuffed egg-halves in a plastic-lined 12-egg carton. Close and refrigerate until time to pack your picnic. Keep the egg carton level when you place it in your picnic cooler.

Serves 6.

Rock Cornish Hens

Prepare the hens the day before. After they are cooked, wrap each one in a coat of plastic wrap and place in the refrigerator. Place the sauce in a bowl, cover with plastic wrap, and refrigerate. The morning of the picnic skim all the fat from the top of the sauce. Reheat sauce before leaving for the picnic.

6 1- to 1½-pound Rock Cornish
    hens
1 tablespoon salt
1 teaspoon pepper
2 tablespoons butter
1 cup dry red wine
1 tablespoon Gravy Master
¼ cup Madeira

Rub the hens with salt and pepper. Melt the butter in a heat-proof casserole large enough to hold them. Place the hens in the casserole breast side down, and pour red wine over them.

Place casserole in preheated 450° oven and roast 30 minutes, turning hens breast side up after the first 10 minutes. Reduce heat to 350° and roast 25 minutes longer, basting frequently with the pan juices. Remove hens from casserole, cool and then, if you like, you can place each one in a small rimmed dish that just holds it. Cover with plastic wrap. Refrigerate.

Add the Gravy Master and the Madeira to the liquid in the casserole. Cook over high heat until liquid is reduced by half. Pour sauce into bowl (not metal), cover, and place in refrigerator.

The day of the picnic, discard the lid of fat congealed on top of the sauce. Pour the sauce into a small pan and bring to a boil. Pour immediately into a wide-mouthed Thermos jug. Let hens come to room temperature.

At the picnic, pour the hot sauce into the individual dishes holding the hens (or into one shallow dish), and let people dunk pieces of their hens in the sauce.

Serves 6.

Marinated Broccoli

1 recipe Oil and Lemon Dressing
    (page 189)
1 onion, finely chopped
1 bunch fresh broccoli (or 2
    10-ounce boxes frozen broccoli
    spears)
Salt and pepper to taste

Make Oil and Lemon Dressing and add to it the finely chopped onion.

Separate and peel broccoli spears. Put into lightly salted boiling water to cover, and cook without a lid, until crisply tender (about 15 minutes). (Or cook frozen broccoli according to package directions.) Drain very well and pat dry with paper towels. Lay spears in a flat, rimmed dish.

Pour dressing over warm broccoli. Cover and refrigerate until departure time. Drain dressing from broccoli and place broccoli in covered flat dish for traveling.

Serves 6.

Fruit in the Hand

Having consumed your bird, finish your picnic with a selection of fruit to eat out of hand. In early springtime grapes and oranges are refreshing, colorful and plentiful. Australia and South Africa send pears and apples from their autumn to us. As summer approaches, peaches, plums, nectarines and cherries appear in our markets. Whatever the seasonable fruit, have plenty of napkins on hand and let your guests choose their own particular delights from your basket.

6 oranges
2 pounds white seedless grapes
    (and/or seasonable fruit
    available)

Cut oranges in quarters, right through the rind. Wash grapes and drain. (Wash and drain any other fruit you may have.) Keep refrigerated until time to pack. If the day is blistering hot keep the chilled fruit in your cooler along with your other food. Fresh fruit is equally good at room temperature.

Serves 6.

A Boating Picnic for Six

Lemonade-rum Tea
Pickled Shrimp
Salade Niçoise with Euphrates Wafers
Strawberries d'Espagne

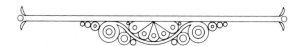

This meal can be eaten on the fantail, in the cabin, drifting along, or tied to a dock. Nothing on the menu needs to be cooked on board, so even if it's a rowboat or a canoe you can enjoy a picnic on the water.

Lemonade-rum Tea

Dark rum has such a pervasive flavor that you need add only a little to zip up rather ordinary iced tea. My husband deserves full credit for evolving this recipe.

20 tea bags
3 quarts boiling water
4 6-ounce cans frozen lemonade
1 tablespoon dark rum per glass, or more, to taste, added at serving time

Make this in 2 batches, in ½-gallon pitchers. Place teabags in pitchers and pour in boiling water. Let stand until desired strength. Fish out tea bags and pour 2 cans slightly defrosted lemonade into each pitcher.

Chill in the refrigerator until time to leave for the boat.

Chill a 1-gallon Thermos jug by filling it full of ice cubes for an hour or two. Dump out ice cubes and replace with lemonade tea. Take the rum bottle along and add rum to each glass in the desired amount at serving time. This saves having to have 2 kinds of tea—plain, and rummy.

Serves 6.

Pickled Shrimp

Use a three-pound peanut butter jar for this. Make at least three days before needed for picnic.

1 medium lemon, thinly sliced
1 large Bermuda onion, thinly sliced
3 pounds shrimp, boiled and peeled
2 bay leaves
1 cup salad oil
2 cups cider vinegar
½ cup pickling spices
1½ tablespoons whole black peppercorns
1 tablespoon sugar
¼ teaspoon mace
1 teaspoon dried ginger
1 tablespoon salt
½ tablespoon dried mustard

Put the sliced lemon and onion in a large jar with a screw top. Add cooked shrimp, bay leaves, and oil. Boil the rest of the ingredients together for 1 minute. Strain into shrimp jar.

Refrigerate, and stir once or twice a day.

Take the shrimp in the jar right along to the picnic in your cooler bag. Have several long-handled pickle forks to spear the shrimp. This is instant food, ready to nibble at the first hunger pang, full of low-calorie, hunger-banishing protein.

Serves 6.

Salade Niçoise with Euphrates Wafers

1 recipe Oil and Vinegar Dressing (page 189)
1 pound green beans, cooked, cut in 1-inch lengths
12-ounce can water-packed tuna fish, drained
1 green pepper, sliced thin
2 stalks celery, sliced thin
6 medium tomatoes, peeled, seeded, and quartered
12 flat anchovies
12 black pitted olives
12 green pitted olives
6 hard-cooked eggs, quartered
½ cup parsley, finely chopped
1 small red onion, sliced in thin rings
½ teaspoon dried basil (or 1 teaspoon fresh)
1 box Euphrates wafers (or sesame crackers)

Make the salad dressing and place in screw-top jar. Refrigerate. Cook beans and cool.

Put the tuna fish in the center of a large salad bowl and arrange clumps of the beans, pepper, celery and tomatoes in a circle around it. Arrange the anchovies like the spokes of a wheel, outlining the vegetables. Circle the rim with two kinds of olives. Garnish with egg quarters, chopped parsley and onion rings. Sprinkle with basil. Cover tightly with plastic wrap and refrigerate until time to pack. Transport to the picnic in cooler bag.

At the picnic, shake the salad dressing jar vigorously and when everyone has seen the gorgeous plate you have unveiled, pour salad dressing over all and toss well just before serving. Pass Euphrates wafers with it.

Serves 6.

Strawberries d'Espagne

It was a skinny Spanish wine merchant who let me in on the orange juice secret—it tastes like some exotic sauce.

3 pints strawberries
2 cups orange juice, freshly squeezed

Clean and hull strawberries, in that order. Put into a bowl (not metal) just big enough to hold them. Pour orange juice over berries. Cover tightly with plastic wrap and set in the refrigerator to marinate for up to 24 hours. An hour before leaving, remove bowl from refrigerator and loosen plastic wrap to let berries breathe a little. Tighten wrap and pack bowl in cooler. Serve berries in paper cups.

Serves 6.

Indoor Picnic for Six

Manhattan Clam Chowder
Chicken Divine
Tossed Green Salad
Fruit Piquant

Sunday afternoons in fall and winter find the group huddled, not around the fire, but gazing deep into the television set. While the bands are marching during the half there is usually a concerted rush to the kitchen to grab a bite to eat. If you, as loving wife, mother or whatever, have the buffet loaded and ready to serve, there is time for a delicious indoor picnic. There are no halves in baseball, bowling or golf; if that's what they're watching, serve the "glassheads" right where they are sitting.

Time your serving according to the sport. During football season, I can be found passing the soup when they give the two-minute warning. This is when the electrically heated tray is a winner—food stays warm without drying out. The soup stays hot in an electric tureen, and the automatic coffee pot insures a steady flow of hot coffee.

Manhattan Clam Chowder

The soup should be made the day before and reheated just before half time. It tastes much better this way.

Serve the soup in mugs and have a basket of oyster crackers (three calories each) on the buffet.

2   slices bacon
1½ tablespoons flour
4   cups water
16-ounce can tomatoes, with their
       juice
1   cup chopped celery
2   or 3 potatoes, chopped (to make
       1 cup)
3   or 4 carrots, chopped (to make
       1 cup)
3   7-ounce cans minced clams and
       juice
½   teaspoon thyme
1   box oyster crackers

Sauté the bacon in a Teflon pan. Set bacon aside to cool, then crumble. Pour off all but 2 tablespoons of the bacon drippings in the pan. Put back over moderate heat, sprinkle in the flour, and keep stirring until the flour browns. Add the water and cook, uncovered, stirring occasionally, until it thickens—about 5 minutes.

Put the rest of the ingredients in a large pot, add the thickened mixture and bring to a boil. Reduce the heat and simmer, covered, 3 hours or more. Serve with oyster crackers. Serves 6.

Chicken Divine

6   whole chicken breasts (12 pieces),
       boned, skinned, and split
Salt, pepper, paprika
3   tablespoons butter
2   12-ounce cans brine-packed
       artichoke hearts
1   pound fresh mushrooms, sliced
2   tablespoons flour
1   cup dry sherry

3   cups Fat-free Chicken Bouillon
       (page 192 or 193)
¼   teaspoon tarragon

Dust chicken breasts with salt, pepper and paprika. Melt the butter in a Teflon pan, add the chicken breasts, and sauté until brown. (Do this in several batches until all are done.)

Cut the browned chicken in 1-inch squares. Place in a casserole you can serve in.

Put the artichokes in a colander and rinse very well in cold water. Drain and pat dry with paper towels. Add to the chicken in the casserole.

Put sliced mushrooms into the same skillet in which you browned the chicken and sauté 5 minutes. Sprinkle in flour; add the sherry and bouillon. Simmer a few minutes, stirring, until thickened. Pour the thickened mushroom sauce over the chicken and artichokes. Cover casserole and put in preheated 350° oven 45 minutes, until bubbling hot.

Serves 6.

Tossed Green Salad

1 recipe American-French Dressing
    (page 191)
1 head iceberg lettuce
1 head romaine
1 head chicory

Make American-French Dressing.

Wash the greens, dry thoroughly, and tear them into bite-size pieces. (*Do not cut.*) Place in salad bowl and keep in refrigerator.

Just before serving, shake salad dressing and pour over greens. Toss well, and place on the buffet for serving.

Serves 6.

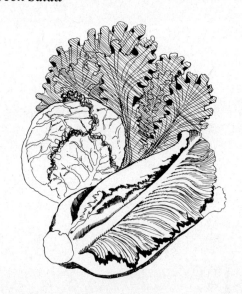

Fruit Piquant

1-pound can calorie-reduced
    peaches
1-pound can water-packed sour red
    cherries
1-pound can calorie-reduced
    apricot halves
1-pound can calorie-reduced pears

½ cup water
¼ cup sugar
Juice of 2 lemons
½ teaspoon ground ginger
½ teaspoon nutmeg
2   cinnamon sticks
4   whole cloves

Drain peaches, cherries and apricots. Place drained fruit in a large ovenproof bowl (not metal). Drain pears and add to fruit in the bowl. Reserve pear liquid.

Mix water, sugar, lemon juice, ginger, nutmeg, and the reserved pear liquid in a pan. Add cinnamon sticks and cloves. Simmer, uncovered, 5 minutes. Strain out cinnamon and cloves and pour liquid over fruit in the bowl.

Let stand at room temperature until dinner time, then heat in the oven with the chicken during its last 20 minutes of cooking.

Serves 6.

CHAPTER SEVEN

Brunches, Lunches and Suppers

*T*hese are informal parties, not too fancy. I mean a checkered tablecloth, perhaps a centerpiece of wild flowers. The menus include hearty, robust dishes, served in various parts of the house or garden instead of sitting formally in the dining room. Soup, salad and dessert is a formula I use often. The time of day often dictates the type of party it will be. Brunch is rarely a formal meal, although you might have a very formal luncheon for important guests. This chapter is about something else. These are the parties that spring up spontaneously: "Come over in the morning for brunch!" "I'll ask everybody back for supper after the show." "Stay for lunch after the committee meeting."

Before you can blithely bid guests to your house, you have to be quite secure about your emergency food supply—on shelf, in freezer or refrigerator. Either that, or know a little delicatessen that never closes. In this chapter I have used eggs in several different ways, all very useful for an impromptu gathering. The ubiquitous ham or Canadian bacon in the refrigerator are well-known staples. Check your cupboards, just for fun, and see what kind of pick-up meal you could bring forth at an hour's notice.

If you are lucky enough to have a big country kitchen, entertain right there. If you are cramped for dining space, use your living room. Improvise. When I was growing up, the teen-age group always sat on the stairs to eat when Mama had her Sunday-night parties. A shady porch is just the place for a cool summer lunch. A card table in front of the fire on a snowy night adds warmth to the gathering.

Be ready when the moment arises—you may never again have the chance to entertain just that magic combination of people. Serve the drinks out of jelly glasses if that is all you have, dish up your delectable victuals on tin plates if you must, just so you have a warm and wonderful party.

What happier entertainment than a Weekend Brunch (page 146)! From Curried Fruit to Coupe de Champagne, this menu means flavor with few calories.

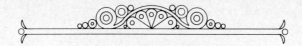

Weekend Brunch for Six

Curried Fruit
Whole Canadian Bacon
Creamed Broccoli en Casserole
Cranberry Bread
Coupe de Champagne

The pantry shelf, refrigerator and freezer hold the ingredients for a super brunch, which means you're always ready to entertain in this most relaxed, delightful way. Cranberry Bread freezes beautifully—stay home the next rainy day and bake a loaf or two. Tuck it in the freezer and be ready at the drop of an invitation.

Curried Fruit

1-pound can calorie-reduced
　　apricots
1-pound can calorie-reduced pears
1-pound can calorie-reduced
　　pineapple chunks
¼ cup peanut oil
1　tablespoon curry powder, or
　　more, to taste
½ cup brown sugar
½ cup white raisins

Drain and reserve fruit, and combine juices. Put oil in an oven-proof casserole (not metal), possibly one that can later come to the table. Add curry powder. Cook 3 minutes over medium heat, stirring. Add brown sugar. Stir in fruit juices, then add reserved fruit and the raisins. Mix well.

Put casserole into a preheated 350° oven and bake 1 hour, uncovered. Serve at once. (If you are doing this ahead of time, cool, cover, and keep in the refrigerator.) Before serving, put casserole into a preheated 350° oven and reheat 15 minutes. Put into a pretty compote dish (or keep in its casserole) and spoon into crystal dishes.

Serves 6.

Whole Canadian Bacon

"Whole" sounds large, but this weighs only about 3 pounds. Any bacon left over goes very well at breakfast, or can be used for eggs Benedict.

3-pound can whole Canadian bacon
½ 7½-ounce jar calorie-reduced
   marmalade
Fresh mint sprigs for garnish
   (optional)

If you have a rotisserie, skewer whole bacon through the center with the rotisserie rod. Paint with marmalade as bacon is turning. Cook about 35 minutes, or until brown and bubbling. Or do it in your oven: place on a rack in a baking pan, coat with marmalade, and bake in a preheated 350° oven 35 or 40 minutes, basting and turning often.

Cut 6 thick slices and place them around the bacon on a serving platter. Garnish with mint sprigs if you like, and bring to the table. Have a sharp knife on hand to slice more as needed.

Serves 6.

Creamed Broccoli en Casserole

6   hard-cooked eggs
2   10-ounce packages frozen
      broccoli spears, cooked
1   teaspoon onion, finely chopped
½   teaspoon dry mustard
2   tablespoons bottled calorie-
      reduced mayonnaise (see
      Appendix)
1   teaspoon Worcestershire sauce
3   tablespoons grated Parmesan
      cheese
Salt and pepper to taste
2   tablespoons butter
1   teaspoon onion, minced
2   tablespoons flour
2   cups skim milk
1   cup sharp cheese, grated
½   teaspoon salt
¼   teaspoon freshly ground black
      pepper
½   teaspoon dry mustard
¼   cup seasoned bread crumbs

Hard-cook eggs, shell and cool. Cook broccoli according to package directions. Drain well on paper towels and reserve.

Slice hard-cooked eggs in half, lengthwise. Scoop out the yolks and mash with chopped onion, mustard, mayonnaise, Worcestershire sauce, grated Parmesan and salt and pepper to taste. Fill the egg whites with stuffing and set aside.

Make cheese sauce as follows. Melt butter in saucepan, add minced onion, and cook until onion is limp and transparent. Add flour and mix well. Add milk and cook, stirring, until sauce thickens enough to coat the spoon (about 5 minutes). Stir in the grated cheese, salt, pepper, and mustard. Cook, stirring, until cheese melts into the sauce.

Arrange the drained, cooked broccoli in 8 by 12-inch baking dish that can come to the table. Place deviled eggs on top of the broccoli, down the middle of the dish, and pour cheese sauce over them. Top with seasoned bread crumbs. Put into a preheated 350° oven and bake 20 minutes, until browned and bubbling.

Serves 6.

Cranberry Bread

This is better prepared the day before, or it can be made weeks ahead and stored in the freezer.

2   cups flour
1   cup sugar
½ teaspoon baking soda
½ teaspoon salt
Juice and grated rind of 1 orange
2   teaspoons butter, melted
Hot water
1   egg, beaten
1   teaspoon vanilla extract
1   cup cranberries, halved
½ cup walnuts, chopped

Preheat oven to 350°.
Sift flour, sugar, baking soda and salt together into a bowl. In a measuring cup put orange juice, grated rind, and melted butter, and add enough hot water to make 1 cup. Stir orange mixture into dry ingredients. Stir in beaten egg and vanilla. Add cranberries and chopped nuts.

Pour into a greased and floured 9 by 5 by 3-inch loaf pan that has the bottom lined with aluminum foil. Put into preheated 350° oven and bake 1 hour. Let stand 24 hours before slicing. Slice thin.

Serves 6.

Coupe de Champagne

3   large ripe peaches
Lemon juice
1   small bunch seedless white
       grapes
½ pint calorie-reduced raspberry
       sherbet
1   bottle pink champagne

Peel, pit and slice peaches. Sprinkle with lemon juice to keep from darkening. Divide slices among six champagne glasses. Add a few white grapes and a small scoop of raspberry sherbet to each glass. Fill up each glass with pink champagne.

Serves 6.

Ladies' Luncheon for Eight

Chicken Bouillon Garnie
Salad Tropicana with Delectable Yogurt Dressing

When ladies meet the talk is often of clothes, which leads to diets, so this delectable combination of low-calorie foods is bound to appeal to everyone. When your guests arrive protesting they can't eat a thing, assure them that you have planned the luncheon with an eye to the calories. Of course, with the chicken reposing in the pineapple, covered with rich-tasting (but calorie-reduced) dressing, no one needs dessert.

Chicken Bouillon Garnie

Whatever kind of bouillon you use, be sure there is no fat on it. Fat is a no-no.

**6 cups double bouillon reserved
    from Salad Tropicana** (page 149)
    (or 5 cups Fat-free Chicken
    Bouillon, page 192 or 193)
**2 pitted black olives, sliced thin,
    for garnish**
2 fresh lemons, quartered

Heat bouillon piping-hot and pour into cups. Float thin slices of pitted black olives on top and serve with lemon quarters for guests to squeeze at will.

Serves 8.

Salad Tropicana with Delectable Yogurt Dressing

I like to simmer chicken breasts in chicken bouillon. I do this the day before, and use the bouillon for the first course—sort of double chicken bouillon.

**5 10½-ounce cans clear chicken
    bouillon**
2 whole chicken breasts (4 pieces)
4 small pineapples
2 oranges
1 large pink grapefruit
Watercress for garnish
8-ounce container vanilla yogurt
1 tablespoon celery seed

First, cook chicken breasts. Heat chicken bouillon in a saucepan. When it boils add chicken breasts, lower heat, and simmer, covered, until just cooked (about 15 minutes). Don't overcook or they will be too

dry and won't slice nicely. Cool the chicken in the bouillon, then remove chicken and cut into thin julienne strips.

(Chill the chicken bouillon in refrigerator. Remove the lid of fat that congeals on top, and there's your defatted chicken bouillon for the first course, above.)

Halve the pineapples, leaving the foliage on top. Cut out cores and remove long sections of flesh to make pineapple spears. Peel and section the oranges and grapefruit. Do this over a bowl to collect the small amount of juices from the fruit. Reserve the juices.

Make a bed of citrus fruits in each pineapple shell and place the julienne chicken on top. Stick the pineapple spears in at an angle. Garnish each plate with watercress sprigs. Serve with yogurt dressing.

To make the delectable yogurt dressing, put vanilla yogurt into a bowl (not metal) and add reserved orange and grapefruit juices and celery seed. Mix well. Chill, and serve in a sauceboat along with the Salad Tropicana.

Serves 8.

After Theater Supper for Six

Scallops Supreme
Tomatoes Florentine
Cucumbers à la Dansk
Fantasy Fruit

So many things nowadays have an "early curtain"—theaters, opera, concerts, or sports events—and it's fun to come home for a little supper afterward and discuss the happening. Start preparations in the morning and you will dazzle your guests as you cook supper before their eyes. Chafing dishes have made a big comeback in the last few years, and it's easy to see why.

Scallops Supreme

3 pounds bay scallops (or sea
    scallops, halved or quartered)
1 cup water
1 cup dry white wine
1 medium onion, finely minced
1 teaspoon parsley, finely minced
1 pound mushrooms, sliced
4 egg yolks, well beaten
1 cup skim milk
3 slices Melba-thin bread, toasted
    and quartered
1 tablespoon butter
2 tablespoons flour
Dash of cayenne (optional)
Salt and pepper to taste
Juice of ½ lemon

Early in the day, wash scallops (and if you are using sea scallops, cut in halves or quarters).

To blanch them, bring water and wine to a full boil in a saucepan. Throw in the scallops. When the water and wine boil up again, take off the heat and drain the scallops, reserving the blanching liquid. Keep drained scallops in a covered bowl (not metal) in the refrigerator until needed.

Mince onion and parsley and reserve. Slice mushrooms and reserve. Beat egg yolks, mix smoothly with the milk, and keep chilled.

When the party is nigh, oven-toast very thin bread—spread slices on aluminum foil placed on oven shelf and toast to the desired shade of brown. Cut in quarters and keep warm.

Melt the butter in the blazer pan of the chafing dish. Add the minced onion and sauté until soft. Add the sliced mushrooms and sauté 3 minutes. Blend in the flour and add 1 cup of the scallop blanching liquid, stirring constantly until the sauce is smooth. Add the minced parsley and a dash of cayenne, and season with salt and pepper. Add scallops and bring to a boil.

Take off the fire. Slowly add a few spoonfuls of the hot sauce to the reserved egg yolk mixture, stirring constantly with a wire whisk. Then very gradually stir the egg-yolk mixture into the hot sauce in the chafing dish. Put back over very low heat, stirring constantly until the sauce has thickened enough to coat the spoon. Do not let it boil.

Squeeze lemon juice over all, and serve over toast points.

Serves 6.

Tomatoes Florentine

I have one of those lovely ovens with a timer that can turn itself on while I am still far away—and that's what I do with this recipe.

6 medium-size ripe tomatoes
1 egg, beaten
¼ teaspoon nutmeg
12-ounce package frozen spinach
    soufflé, thawed

Remove ½-inch from stem end of tomatoes, scoop out insides, and drain well.

Beat the egg with the nutmeg and mix into the thawed spinach soufflé.

Stuff tomatoes with the spinach mixture. Place stuffed tomatoes in 11-inch oval oven-proof serving dish.

Put into a preheated 350° oven and bake 35 minutes.

Variation:

Use 2 9-ounce packages frozen creamed spinach (instead of spinach soufflé) and proceed as above.

Serves 6.

Cucumbers à la Dansk

3 large cucumbers
¾ teaspoon salt
1 teaspoon sugar
¼ cup white vinegar
Freshly ground black pepper
Fresh dill, finely chopped (or dill
    weed) **to taste**

Thinly peel cucumbers with a vegetable peeler, leaving a bit of the skin on. Score lengthwise with the tines of a table fork. Halve the cucumbers lengthwise and remove the seeds. Cut in thin slices across, put into a bowl (not metal), and sprinkle with salt. Cover and refrigerate overnight, if you like (one hour is enough, though).

Drain well, and pat dry with paper towels. Put drained cucumbers into a pretty crystal serving dish, sprinkle with sugar, and pour vinegar over them. Sprinkle with pepper and dill to taste. Serve chilled.

Serves 6.

Fantasy Fruit

2-ounce package (2 envelopes)
    calorie-reduced lemon-flavor
    gelatin
3 cups boiling water
Few drops green food coloring
3 drops peppermint flavoring
12-ounce package frozen melon
    balls, thawed
1 cup seedless white grapes
1 pint strawberries
Fresh mint sprigs for garnish

Make lemon gelatin, using only 3 cups boiling water (instead of 4). Mix in food coloring and peppermint flavoring, place in a bowl (not metal), and put in the refrigerator to chill. When partially set (in about 1 hour) stir in melon balls and grapes. Place in a 1-quart mold and chill until firm.

Rinse and drain strawberries well on paper towels, but do not hull (their green leaves will look pretty at serving time). Chill until needed.

Before serving (you can do this before you leave for the theater), unmold (as directed on page 117). Decorate with clumps of strawberries and sprigs of fresh mint. Cover with plastic wrap and refrigerate until serving time.

Serves 6.

Cold Weather Brunch for Six

Pink Grapefruit
Scrambled Eggs sans Beurre with Deviled Bread Sticks
Stuffed Onions
Apricot Fluff

We have brunch parties often in cool weather. We have a delicious substantial, low-calorie meal like this one that will sustain us all until supper, no matter what the afternoon activities happen to be. Brunch leaves time in the short daylight hours for things like a strenuous game of touch football, skating, bowling, museum visiting, an invigorating walk up the avenue or through the park, or even just snuggling closer to the fire, finishing the crossword puzzle.

Pink Grapefruit

3 large pink grapefruit
1 pint strawberries
½ cup orange juice
1 teaspoon sugar

Cut grapefruit in half. Section them well and remove seeds. Set aside and chill. Rinse strawberries and pat dry; hull and slice.

Put orange juice into a bowl (not metal) and dissolve sugar in it. Add the strawberries and let them marinate in the sweetened orange juice until serving time. Spoon the berries and their juice over the grapefruit.

Serves 6.

Scrambled Eggs sans Beurre

These eggs taste so good no one suspects that there is no butter at all in them.

12 eggs
¼ cup skim milk
½ teaspoon salt
½ teaspoon white pepper

Put everything in the blender and blend at high speed for 1 minute.

Heat a Teflon skillet over a moderate flame. When just hot, pour in egg mixture. Cook, stirring constantly, until eggs are set.

Serve at once, on a heated platter. Serves 6.

Deviled Bread Sticks

You can do this with regular bread sticks, but the little skinny imported Grissini are best.

2   tablespoons butter
1   clove garlic, pressed
¼ cup Worcestershire sauce
4-ounce box imported thin bread
    sticks
1   teaspoon salt (coarse is best)

Preheat oven to 250°.

Put butter, garlic, and Worcestershire sauce in a skillet over moderate heat and stir until butter is melted and all is nicely hot. Do not cook.

Remove from fire and paint bread sticks with the hot butter with a pastry brush. Place bread sticks on a cookie sheet and sprinkle with the coarse salt. Put into preheated 250° oven and bake 45 minutes, until crisp and dry. Serve hot, with scrambled eggs.

Serves 6.

Stuffed Onions

These may be prepared the day before.

12   large white onions
4½-ounce can deviled ham
½   teaspoon catsup
½   teaspoon Dijon-type mustard
6   sprigs parsley (or fresh dill)

Parboil the onions. Cool and scoop out centers (as directed on page 73).

Combine deviled ham, catsup and mustard. Stuff into onions. Garnish each with a sprig of parsley or fresh dill.

Set on a pretty plate, cover with plastic wrap, and chill until serving time.

Serves 6.

Apricot Fluff

12 ounces dried apricots (to make
    1½ cups)
3   **slices lemon**
6   **egg whites**
2   **tablespoons superfine sugar**

Put apricots in a saucepan with water to cover, add lemon slices, and simmer, covered, until soft (about 20 minutes). Drain off all but ½ cup of the juice.

Place drained apricots and the ½ cup of juice in a blender for 2 minutes at high speed, or purée through a sieve.

Beat the egg whites with the sugar until stiff. Then fold puréed apricots into beaten egg whites.

Pile into a lightly greased 1-quart soufflé dish. Put into a preheated 350° oven and bake, 30 minutes, while you are eating the first part of the brunch.

Serves 6.

Nuncheon, Regency Style, for Six

Vegetable Cocktail with Celery Swizzles
Ham Mousse
Green Bean Salad
Fruit-filled Oranges

"Nuncheon" is a word that has been out of use for about one hundred and fifty years. It turns out to be a perfect little cold lunch (like this one) to be eaten in the gazebo, sun porch, or terrace, in the most informal way. It's easy to do, and nice when you have houseguests you want to impress—especially if you're feeding them three times a day!

Vegetable Cocktail with Celery Swizzles

Chill whiskey-sour glasses in the freezer and no ice cubes are needed.

24 ounces vegetable juice cocktail,
    chilled
6   **leafy-topped small inner celery**
    stalks

Chill glasses in the freezer. At serving time, fill the glasses with chilled vegetable juice cocktail and put a celery swizzle in each glass.

Serves 6.

Ham Mousse

1   envelope unflavored gelatin
¼   cup cold water
1½   cups Fat-free Chicken Bouillon
        (page 192 or 193)
2   pounds cooked ground ham
¼   cup chopped celery
1   tablespoon onion, grated
½   cup Calorie-reduced Mayon-
        naise (page 187)
1   teaspoon Worcestershire sauce
¼   teaspoon pepper
Dash cayenne (optional)

Soak gelatin in ¼ cup cold water to soften. Dissolve softened gelatin in 1½ cups boiling chicken bouillon.

Place in a bowl (not metal) and chill until nearly set.

Grind cooked ham with the finest blade of the grinder. Add celery, grated onion and mayonnaise to ham, and season with Worcestershire, pepper, and cayenne.

Combine ham mixture with nearly set gelatin and pour into a lightly oiled 6-cup ring mold. Place in the refrigerator and chill until firm.

Unmold (as directed on page 117) onto a chilled plate, and fill center with the Green Bean Salad.
Serves 6.

Green Bean Salad

Sunflower kernels (available at health-food stores) add a little nutty crunch to the beans.

1   recipe Oil and Lemon Dressing
       (page 189)
3   10-ounce packages frozen cross-
       cut beans
¼ cup sunflower kernels

Make Oil and Lemon Dressing. Cook green beans as directed on package. Drain and immediately

pour salad dressing over them. Sprinkle with sunflower kernels. Place in a bowl (not metal) and chill in the refrigerator.

When Ham Mousse is unmolded on its chilled platter, drain the beans and heap them in the center of the ring mold.
Serves 6.

Fruit-filled Oranges

6   large navel oranges
1   apple, peeled, cored and diced
2   peaches, peeled and sliced
¾ cup fresh pineapple, peeled and
       diced
2   pears, peeled and diced

¼ cup crumbled stale macaroons
¼ cup orange-flavored liqueur
¾ cup calorie-reduced raspberry
       syrup (see Appendix)
6   small scoops vanilla ice milk

Cut 1 inch off top of each orange. Hollow out, reserving some of the pulp.

Prepare apple, peaches, pineapple, and pears. Put into a bowl and mix with small pieces of the reserved orange pulp. Add crumbled macaroons. Put fruit mixture into orange shells.

Stir the orange liqueur into the raspberry syrup, and dribble over the fruit. Put a small scoop of vanilla ice milk on top of each orange shell and serve at once.

Serves 6.

Sunday Night Supper for Six

Gazpacho with Shrimp
Cheese Soufflé
Endive and Mushroom Salad
Double Lemon Ice

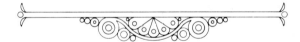

This simply elegant meal is perfect for a Sunday night, calorie-reduced but still hearty and well flavored. Soufflés are beautiful, and I assure you, *easy* to do. Where they ever got the reputation for being difficult I do not know.

Gazpacho with Shrimp

The original recipe for gazpacho calls for bread and croutons. This recipe adds protein with the shrimp while reducing calories.

3 hard-cooked eggs
2 tablespoons olive oil
1 clove garlic, pressed
1 teaspoon dry mustard
1 teaspoon Worcestershire sauce
½ cup green pepper, finely chopped
½ cup scallions, finely chopped

5 cups tomato juice
Juice of 2 lemons
½ pound cooked medium shrimp, halved
Dash Tabasco sauce (optional)
Salt and pepper to taste

Hard-boil the eggs and mash yolks. (Finely chop the whites and reserve for garnish.) Mix olive oil into mashed yolks. Add garlic, mustard, Worcestershire sauce, chopped green pepper and scallions. Pour in tomato juice and lemon juice and mix well. Fold in the cooked shrimp. Season with Tabasco and salt and pepper to taste.

Serve iced in individual soup bowls, with the finely chopped egg white for garnish.

Serves 6.

Cheese Soufflé

You know soufflés—how they won't wait for anybody? I put my soufflé in the oven just after the last guest arrives. This gives us time to have a drink and eat our soup before the soufflé is ready.

2   tablespoons butter
2   tablespoons flour
2   cups skim milk
1   tablespoon Worcestershire sauce
6   ounces grated cheese (American, Swiss, or Parmesan)
1   teaspoon dried mustard
½   teaspoon salt
¼   teaspoon white pepper
6   eggs, separated

Melt butter in saucepan and stir in flour until well blended. Stir in milk and Worcestershire sauce and heat, stirring constantly with a wire whisk, until sauce thickens enough to coat the whisk (about 5 minutes). Add grated cheese and stir until cheese melts. Add seasonings.

Beat egg yolks in a cup. Stir in a spoonful or two of the hot cheese mixture. Take the cheese mixture off the fire and slowly stir into it the egg yolks until smoothly blended. Let mixture cool.

Beat egg whites until stiff. (They beat better if they are at room temperature.) Fold egg whites *gently* into egg mixture. Turn into a 6-cup soufflé dish (or any straight-sided oven-proof dish).

Put into a preheated 350° oven and bake 45 minutes to 1 hour, until puffed and brown but still a little moist inside. It should go instantly from oven to table.

Serves 6.

Endive and Mushroom Salad

This salad works out well when you are serving a soufflé because it can be placed on the table when you sit down at the beginning of the meal. The dressing is placed on the salad well in advance.

½ pound raw mushrooms
Juice of 2 lemons
6   Belgian endive, cut in rounds
½ cup celery, finely chopped
1   tablespoon chives, chopped
½ teaspoon salt
¼ teaspoon freshly ground black
      pepper
A pinch of dried savory
3   tablespoons olive oil

Trim the ends off the mushrooms, leaving stems on, and slice down through the caps and stems. Put into salad bowl and pour the lemon juice over at once to keep them from turning dark.

Slice endive into ½-inch rounds, separate the rings, and add to the bowl. Add the rest of the ingredients and toss well. Chill in refrigerator until serving time. Toss once again just before serving.

Serves 6.

Double Lemon Ice

Italian water ice can be used, if you live near an Italian section. This recipe is really lemon-y!

½   2-ounce package (1 envelope)
      calorie-reduced lemon
      gelatin dessert
2½ cups boiling water for the lemon
      gelatin
Grated rind and juice of 3 lemons
      (or more, to give ½ cup juice)

Dissolve the lemon gelatin in the boiling water. Grate the rind off lemons and then squeeze them. (You will probably need three lemons to get enough juice, depending on size.) Add lemon juice to lemon gelatin, pour into an ice tray, and place in the freezer. Freeze until nearly firm.

Scrape out into a chilled bowl and beat with chilled beater until smooth. Return beaten lemon-ice to freezer and freeze until hard.

At serving time, divide among 6 crystal dessert dishes and garnish with the grated lemon rind.

Serves 6.

CHAPTER EIGHT

Holiday Parties

The holidays roll around more quickly with each passing year, it seems. We always wind up the season fatter than we began. Not to worry! All the gaiety, joy and happiness of a festive occasion can still be yours. Your knowledge and planning of calorie-reduced food can add to the pleasures of party times—and while you are feasting you will know that you won't have to be fasting later in the week.

You are the hostess, and in that role you can plan simple, conservative food within the framework of tradition. You can keep the calories out and the flavor and richness in by substituting less heavy food in the menus. Your Thanksgiving table will still look like a groaning board, but many fattening items will have been tactfully, and quietly, left out.

Offering vast amounts of fattening food has gone out of style. You can serve sufficient quantities so that those who wish to can go back for seconds. The dieter's restraint must come from within, but must your company know that Hubbard squash and brussels sprouts are lots less caloric than mashed potatoes and creamed onions? The hostess can control the basic ingredients for any holiday meal, be it Thanksgiving, Christmas, Chanukah, New Year's Eve or Washington's Birthday. The guest controls the amount he consumes.

When you are faced with a large group for a holiday party, prepare as much in advance as possible. Freezers are a tremendous help here. Shopping can often be completed a week or ten days before, keeping you out of crowded markets at the last minute. Spend the saved time making a beautiful flower arrangement for your table. I have noted the recipes that can be prepared ahead of time.

A Thanksgiving turkey (page 179) has traditional but non-fattening trimmings such as Marco Polo Dressing, Scalloped Oysters, Pumpkin Soufflé.

161

Old-fashioned Tree Trimming Party for Eight

Onion Soup
New Orleans Shrimp
Deviled Fish Cakes with Cucumber Sauce
Scandihoovian Meatballs
Finger Salad
Christmas Cookies

Sing a carol, trim the tree. . . . This is a party for all ages. Nobody believes anymore that Santa does all the work, though the little ones cling firmly to their belief in the jolly fat man. I plan the tree trimming party for the weekend before the holiday, and invite people to come at four o'clock and stay on for supper. The food is prepared in advance because things can get hectic. Set the tree up too—firmly, well anchored—before the guests arrive. Have the boxes of ornaments and trimmings ready for action. Have the soup ready early—even in this day of the overheated car people coming in from the cold like a steaming hot cup to warm them. Serve the soup from an electric tureen in mugs for convenience.

Onion Soup

Do this ahead.

3   pounds onions
4   tablespoons butter
2   tablespoons olive oil
Salt and pepper to taste
1/3 teaspoon nutmeg
2   cloves garlic, pressed
3   tablespoons flour
1   cup dry white wine
12 cups Fat-free Beef Bouillon
     (page 192 or 193)

Slice onions very thin and sauté them in butter and oil until they are soft but *not* burned. Season with salt, pepper, and nutmeg. Add garlic, and stir in flour until well blended. Add the wine, stir well, then add the bouillon. Cover and simmer 45 minutes.

Set out in a fine tureen or marmite with a ladle. Surround with mugs and let people help themselves.

Serves 8.

New Orleans Shrimp

This is really very juicy, almost like a gumbo, so I serve it in little bowls.

2   slices bacon, chopped
4   onions, diced
9-ounce package frozen okra,
    thawed
3   cups hot water
1   cup canned tomatoes, chopped
    up, with their juice
½ cup celery, chopped
1   green pepper, chopped
2   cloves, garlic, pressed
Salt and pepper to taste
½ teaspoon dried thyme
3   pounds uncooked shrimp, peeled
    and cleaned
1   teaspoon gumbo filé powder
3   tablespoons chopped parsley

Sauté the bacon in a Teflon skillet until nearly crisp. Pour off fat from the skillet and drain bacon on paper towels.

Add onions and okra to the same skillet and sauté 5 minutes, stirring frequently. Stir in the hot water, chopped tomatoes, celery and green pepper, garlic, salt, pepper and thyme.

Add the shrimp. Simmer 10 minutes. Off the fire, just before serving, stir in the filé powder, mix well, and sprinkle parsley over all.

Serves 8.

Deviled Fish Cakes with Cucumber Sauce

If you have more than one chafing dish (doesn't everyone?) you can sauté the fish cakes right at the table. But I find them easier to do in the kitchen and hold on an electric serving tray, with the sauce beside them.

2   pounds halibut or cod, cooked
    and flaked (to make 4 cups)
2   8-ounce cans calorie-reduced
    cream of mushroom soup
1   teaspoon dry mustard
Dash of cayenne (optional)
1   tablespoon parsley, finely
    chopped
3   egg yolks
½ cup dry seasoned bread crumbs
1   whole egg beaten with 1
    tablespoon water
4   tablespoons butter

1   cucumber, peeled, seeded and
    diced
1   onion, finely chopped
1   tablespoon parsley, finely
    chopped
2   cups tomato pulp, canned (or
    4 medium tomatoes, peeled,
    seeded and diced)
½ teaspoon paprika
Salt and pepper to taste
¼ teaspoon freshly ground black
    pepper
1   tablespoon tarragon vinegar

Put fish into boiling salted water, lower the flame and simmer, covered, just until it loses that transparent look and flakes easily. Do not overcook. Lift out of the poaching liquid; cool, then flake.

Combine the mushroom soup with mustard, cayenne, parsley, flaked fish and egg yolks. Mix well and put into a bowl (not metal); cover and put in refrigerator. When fish mixture is thoroughly chilled, form into cakes about 2½ inches in diameter.

Put bread crumbs in a saucer. Beat the egg with the water and place in another saucer. Dip fish cakes first into the crumbs, then into the egg, and again into the crumbs. Do this early in the day (or at least an hour before dinner). Put coated fish cakes on a flat dish, cover with plastic wrap, and chill until cooking time.

To finish the fish cakes, put butter in a Teflon skillet over medium heat. When butter sizzles, add fish cakes, a few at a time, and sauté until nicely golden (about 2 minutes per side). Keep warm on an electric hot tray with cucumber sauce beside them.

To make cucumber sauce, combine in a saucepan the cucumber, onion, parsley, tomato pulp, paprika, salt and pepper. Simmer, covered 20 minutes. Take off the stove, add the tarragon vinegar, and stir well. Pour into a warmed sauce boat and keep hot beside the fish cakes.

Serves 8.

Scandihoovian Meatballs

2 slices rye bread, crumbled
½ cup skim milk
1 medium onion, finely chopped
1½ pounds lean ground beef, ground twice
1 egg
1 teaspoon salt
¼ teaspoon freshly ground black pepper
1 tablespoon butter
½ cup water
1 tablespoon cider vinegar
4 tablespoons catsup
2 tablespoons calorie-reduced maple syrup
1 tablespoon cornstarch
¼ cup water
Parsley, finely chopped, for garnish

Crumble the rye bread into the milk. Add onion, beef, egg, salt and pepper. Shape into about 24 meatballs slightly smaller than a walnut. (If you dip your hands in cold water the job is easier.)

Melt butter in a Teflon skillet and brown meat on all sides. Mix ½ cup water, vinegar, catsup and maple syrup together and pour over browned meatballs. Stir gently and cook over low heat for 20 minutes.

Stir the cornstarch into ¼ cup

water, and add to sauce. Stir gently to mix in well and continue cooking until sauce thickens and becomes clear.

Place the meatballs and sauce in your chafing dish, garnish with parsley and serve with toothpicks nearby.

Serves 8.

Finger Salad

Prepare vegetables the day before—you don't want to be hanging over the sink slicing when all the fun is going on treeside. Plastic bags are the biggest help in keeping everything crisp and cold until serving time.

6 carrots, peeled and sliced into
 sticks
1 cauliflower, broken into flowerets
2 pint boxes cherry tomatoes
2 bunches radishes
2 bunches celery, cut into sticks
3 green peppers, cut into strips

Clean and prepare everything, put into plastic bags, and chill. At serving time arrange in pretty groups of contrasting colors on a large round plate with the cauliflower in the middle.

Serves 8.

Christmas Cookies

Everybody, absolutely everybody, has a special Christmas cookie, or even more than one special cookie. Certain friends always bring a box of home-made cookies during the holidays; Edie makes sugar cookies like the ones my grandmother made; Ann-Marie is hooked on bourbon balls; our German sitter, Elisabeth, brings Pfeffernüsse. I have been experimenting and have come up with some pretty tasty cinnamon cookies, and I also have a refrigerator cookie we're all fond of.

Cinnamon Cookies

5   tablespoons butter
1   egg, beaten
1   cup all-purpose flour
½ teaspoon baking powder
2   teaspoons vanilla extract
2   tablespoons cinnamon
2   tablespoons sugar

Cream the butter, add the beaten egg, then add flour and baking powder. Mix together with an electric beater at low speed for 3 minutes. Add vanilla. Sprinkle 1 tablespoon of the cinnamon over dough and mix in slightly. Form dough into balls about 1 inch in diameter.

Mix sugar and the remaining tablespoon of cinnamon in a small bowl and roll dough balls in it to coat them. Put dough balls on a Teflon cookie sheet. Press each one flat with the tines of a table fork that has been dipped in cold water. Bake 15 minutes in a preheated 375° oven. Let stand 2 minutes, then remove with a spatula to a wire rack to cool.

Makes about 36 cookies.

Refrigerator Cookies

4   tablespoons butter
2   tablespoons dark-brown sugar
1   egg, beaten
½ 2-ounce package (1 envelope) calorie-reduced vanilla pudding
1   cup all-purpose flour
½ teaspoon baking powder
Pinch of salt
½ teaspoon vanilla extract

First cream the butter with the brown sugar, working well with wooden spoon until fluffy. Stir in the lightly beaten egg until blended. Then add the rest of the ingredients except vanilla. Mix well, add vanilla, and mix well again. Form dough into a roll, wrap in plastic wrap, and chill 30 minutes (or overnight) in refrigerator.

At baking time, cut roll in ⅛-inch slices. Place slices 2 inches apart on a Teflon cookie sheet and put in a preheated 375° oven 8 to 10 minutes.

Remove cookies from oven, let sit for a minute, then transfer with a spatula to a rack to cool.

Makes 24 cookies.

Variation:

Substitute chocolate pudding for the vanilla pudding for a change of flavor.

New Year's Eve Buffet for Sixteen

Herring in Wine
Ham and Asparagus Rolls
Roast Beef with Mustard Sauce
Oven-crisped Chicken Legs with Plum Sauce
Cucumber Salad
Coleslaw
Compote of Poached Fruit

This sort of party is much appreciated by the young married group, especially those with children. The party can begin as late as 10 P.M., after all the little and not so little ones are safe in bed. As food will be served right after midnight, you really don't need canapés, dips, or other unnecessary temptations. Too much food early can dampen your party so it never gets off the ground. Concentrate on your midnight buffet. Follow it with Sanka, coffee, or continued drinks for the determined celebrators.

Herring in Wine

Good luck to tear a herring at midnight! Be sure to get herring in wine, not in sour cream. Store in refrigerator for at least two days before using.

4 8-ounce jars herring in wine sauce
4 onions, sliced
6 stalks celery, sliced crosswise
2 sweet red peppers, sliced in strips
Juice of 2 lemons

Empty herring into large bowl (not metal). Slice the onions, celery and red peppers. Add to the herring in the bowl. Add lemon juice and mix well together.

Serve in a crystal bowl. Don't forget small plates and forks just for this, so everything else won't get fishy.

Serves 16.

Ham and Asparagus Rolls

4 8-ounce cans white asparagus tips
2 pounds baked ham, thinly sliced
Dijon-type mustard
Parsley sprigs

Spread each slice of ham thinly with Dijon mustard. Drain asparagus tips and pat dry with paper towels.

Place one drained asparagus tip at the end of each slice of ham and roll up tightly. Place in diagonal rows on a silver platter. Garnish with parsley sprigs. Cover with plastic wrap and refrigerate until serving time.
Serves 16.

Roast Beef with Mustard Sauce

For this you roast a delicious boneless rolled sirloin of beef. Make it early in the day and let it cool to room temperature. Slice it thin, just before serving time, and the juices will run with the knife.

5-pound rolled beef roast
Salt
Freshly ground black pepper
1 clove garlic
1 tablespoon olive oil
½ tablespoon butter
1 onion, finely chopped
1 carrot, finely chopped
2 cloves garlic, finely chopped
3 tablespoons flour
10½-ounce can beef bouillon
½ cup red wine
2 anchovies, chopped
¼ teaspoon Tabasco
2 tablespoons Dijon-type mustard
Salt and pepper to taste

Rub the beef with salt and pepper. Cut garlic clove in half and rub meat with it. Then score the coating of fat. Put into a preheated 325° oven and roast 20 minutes per pound, for rare, basting occasionally with pan drippings. Set aside to cool.
Just before serving, cut into thin slices. Season the slices with salt and pepper and roll neatly into fingers. Place like spokes of a wheel around a platter holding a dish of mustard sauce in the center.

To make the mustard sauce, heat oil and butter in Teflon saucepan. Sauté onions until limp, add carrots and garlic, and continue sautéing until the vegetables are soft and slightly brown. Stir in flour with a whisk and add bouillon and red wine. Add anchovies, Tabasco, mustard, salt and pepper and continue cooking over low heat until sauce thickens.

Place half the sauce in a blender and blend 1 minute at medium speed. Put in a covered pint jar. Blend the other half and add it to the jar. Mix well, cover, and place in refrigerator to cool until serving time.
Serves 16.

Oven-crisped Chicken Legs with Plum Sauce

Make up your own crumb coating, saving money and calories. Use Skinny Shake coating—it adds only about 50 calories per serving, compared to 200 for deep-fat frying.

1 recipe Skinny Shake (page 191)
32 chicken legs (without second
      joints)
1-pound can calorie-reduced
      purple plums, with juice
1 tablespoon soy sauce
1 tablespoon honey
1 tablespoon cornstarch
¼ cup cold water

Make 1 recipe Skinny Shake.

Put chicken legs, a few at a time, in a plastic bag with Skinny Shake coating, and shake hard. Place coated chicken legs on Teflon cookie sheets. Put chicken into preheated 375° oven and bake 45 minutes, turning once.

To make the plum sauce, pit plums and place them in a blender with their juice, soy sauce and honey. Blend well, in 2 or 3 batches, so you won't overload the blender, at high speed for 2 minutes.

Place blended plum mixture in saucepan and bring slowly to the boiling point. Dissolve cornstarch in ¼ cup cold water and stir into the plums. Simmer, stirring, until sauce is glossy and thickens enough to coat spoon.

Pile hot crisped chicken legs on a rimmed serving dish, with the plum sauce beside it. Keep both warm on an electric tray. Plenty of paper napkins are needed here.

Serves 16.

Cucumber Salad

1½ packages (3 envelopes)
      calorie-reduced lime-flavored
      gelatin
3   cups boiling water
16-ounce can crushed pineapple
      (unsweetened) and ½ cup of
      its juice
½   teaspoon salt
2   cups cucumber, peeled, seeded
      and diced
1   tablespoon vinegar
1   tablespoon lemon juice
Chicory leaves for garnish
4-ounce can pimientos for garnish

Place gelatin in a large bowl (not metal). Stir boiling water into gelatin until dissolved. Drain pineapple and reserve. Add ½ cup of the pineapple juice and salt to bowl. Cool gelatin in refrigerator until slightly soupy.

Mix in the pineapple, cucumber, vinegar and lemon juice. Pour mixture into a 7-cup mold. Refrigerate until firm.

Unmold (as directed on page 117), onto a silver serving dish. Garnish with curly chicory leaves, and strips of pimientos laid out to look like bows.

Serves 16.

Coleslaw

This is a very crisp, low-fat coleslaw.

2 large heads cabbage, finely
   shredded
2 Bermuda onions, thinly sliced
2 raw carrots, shredded
2 green peppers, shredded
2 cups white vinegar
4 tablespoons salad oil
2 tablespoons sugar

1 teaspoon black pepper, freshly
   ground
2 teaspoons salt

Toss all ingredients together in a large bowl. Place in refrigerator to crisp.
Serves 16.

Compote of Poached Fruit

16-ounce can calorie-reduced
   black cherries, pitted
16-ounce can calorie-reduced pears
2 8-ounce packages dried apricots
12-ounce package dried mixed fruit
1 pound dried prunes
2 lemons, quartered
8-ounce carton calorie-reduced sour
   cream

Drain cherries and pears and reserve. Put the cherry and pear juice in a large saucepan with the dried apricots, mixed fruit and prunes. Add enough water to cover fruit. Bring to a boil, lower heat and simmer, covered, until the fruit is tender (about 20 to 30 minutes). Carefully mix in the reserved cherries and pears, and turn into a crystal bowl.

This can be served warm or at room temperature. Have a bowl of calorie-reduced sour cream close by for those who want it.
Serves 16.

Washington's Birthday Dinner for Eight

Bouillon Printanière
Duckling en Papillote
Chived Carrots
Broccoli Vinaigrette
Cherries Flambée

I like to have a birthday party for the father of our country—he's sort of noncontroversial these days, and that's a help. It seems toward the middle of February that spring will never come, and everyone who can be is off on some tropical island except me. It's fun to round up the stay-at-homes and have a swinging party.

Bouillon Printanière

6 radishes
½ cucumber
½ small zucchini
½ small carrot
3 small inner stalks celery
8 cups Fat-free Chicken Bouillon
    (page 192 or 193)

Cut vegetables into transparent-thin rounds. They must be very fresh and crisp. Put into tureen, pour boiling bouillon over them, and serve at once.

Serves 8.

Duckling en Papillote

I know that duck has a reputation for being fattening and over-rich. Not so. Here the cooking method makes the difference. There are tricks to all trades, and this is one of my favorite low-calorie sleights-of-hand.

The recipe can be prepared the day before except for the last 35 minutes in the oven.

2 3½- to 4-pound ducklings, thawed
2 tablespoons drippings from ducks
2 tablespoons flour
½ teaspoon salt
2 scallions, finely chopped
1 teaspoon thyme
½ teaspoon chervil
½ teaspoon rosemary
½ teaspoon sage
1 teaspoon fresh parsley, finely chopped
1 teaspoon prepared mustard
2 cups dry white wine

Truss ducklings' wings and legs to body so they don't spread awkwardly during cooking. To help fat escape, prick skin (not flesh) all over at ½-inch intervals. If you have a rotisserie, skewer and roast at moderate heat (350°) 45 minutes. If not, set ducklings in a roasting pan on a rack or trivet (to keep them above dripping fat) and roast 45 minutes in a preheated 350° oven.

Ducklings will be lightly browned and will have given up most of their fat. Discard all fat except 2 tablespoons. Cut ducklings in quarters with kitchen shears and set aside in a warm place.

Put 2 tablespoons duck drippings in a Teflon pan over a moderate flame. Scatter in flour and mix well.

Add salt, scallions, herbs, parsley, mustard and white wine. Simmer, stirring constantly, for a few minutes until you have a smooth sauce. Place the duckling quarters on individual pieces of heavy aluminum foil, large enough to fold over with a "drug-store fold." Pour 2 tablespoons sauce over each quarter. Fold aluminum foil around them into leakproof packages, or papillotes.

(If the papillotes are prepared in advance, hold in refrigerator. Take them out in time to return to room temperature; otherwise increase the baking time by 15 minutes.)

Preheat oven to 450°. Place ducklings in oven and reduce heat at once to 325°. Bake 35 minutes. Serve each guest an unopened papillote. When the papillote is opened there will be a fantastic aroma.

Serves 8.

Chived Carrots

2 bunches carrots (or 2 16-ounce cans)
Salt to taste
2 tablespoons chopped chives, fresh or frozen

Cook carrots, whole or sliced, in boiling water to cover until tender. Drain well. (Or heat canned carrots in their juice and drain.) Salt to taste.

Sprinkle drained carrots with chopped chives and mix well to distribute the chives. Put into a heated serving dish and serve with the duckling.

Serves 8.

Broccoli Vinaigrette

The advantage of serving cold broccoli is that you can cook it the day before and the house won't smell the day of the party. Also, it makes this delicious salad.

1 recipe Oil and Lemon Dressing (page 189)
1 small red onion, minced fine
3 small radishes, minced fine
1 teaspoon prepared horseradish
½ teaspoon prepared mustard (Dijon-type, preferably)
1 gherkin, minced fine
2 bunches fresh broccoli, stems peeled (or 3 10-ounce packages frozen broccoli spears)
Salt

Make Oil and Lemon Dressing. Add to it the onion, radishes, horseradish, mustard, and gherkin and shake well in a screw-top jar. Chill.

Cook broccoli in boiling salted water to cover, being careful not to overcook it and lose its lovely color. Drain well, then chill.

Put broccoli on individual salad plates, and spoon on dressing (about 2 tablespoons per serving).

Serves 8.

Cherries Flambée

2   16-ounce cans calorie-reduced
    pitted Bing cherries (or 2
    pounds fresh Bing cherries,
    pitted)
½   cup sugar
½   teaspoon cinnamon
Dash nutmeg
½   cup Cherry Heering
1½ pints vanilla ice milk

Drain the cherries, reserving 1 cup of the cherry juice. (If you are using fresh cherries, poach them in 1 cup water, flavored with ½ teaspoon vanilla. Drain, and reserve 1 cup of the juice.) To the reserved juice add sugar, cinnamon and nutmeg.

Place the cherries in the blazer pan of your chafing dish and pour the juice over them. Put over a low flame and keep it warm, just under a simmer—this must warm slowly.

Place a scoop of ice milk in each of 8 sherbet glasses. Heat the liqueur in a small saucepan (or in a soup ladle held over the kitchen fire). Pour heated liqueur over cherries and set alight. As the flames die, spoon cherries and their liquid over the ice milk and serve at once.

Serves 8.

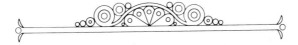

Easter Dinner for Eight

Consommé Madrilène à la Russe
Rolled Roast of Lamb with Apricot Filling
Spinach Ring with Onions
Rabbit Food
Lemon Ice Box Charlotte

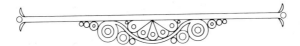

All the wonder of new beginnings comes to the world at Easter. There is a freshness to the spring days that makes everyone rejoice; the bitterness of winter is past, and life is renewed. There are many traditional foods associated with the Easter season. As a change from ham, I often serve lamb.

Lamb that has been boned, stuffed, and rolled is much easier to carve than a leg, and as we often have a crisis at carving time, this is my way of solving the problem. Use the colored eggs collected by the children for a centerpiece.

Consommé Madrilène à la Russe

4 12-ounce cans consommé
    madrilène
8 tablespoons calorie-reduced sour
    cream
8 teaspoons red or black caviar

Heat consommé until hot, but not boiling. Pour into consommé cups. Top each serving with one tablespoonful sour cream, and carefully place one teaspoonful of caviar on each spoonful of cream.
Serves 8.

Rolled Roast of Lamb with Apricot Filling

8-ounce package dried apricot
    halves
2 tablespoons lemon juice
1 teaspoon salt
1 cup water
5-ounce can water chestnuts,
    drained and diced
4 tablespoons butter at room
    temperature
½ teaspoon garlic powder
½ 8-ounce package herbed bread
    stuffing
7-pound leg of lamb, boned,
    trimmed of fat (reserve bones)

Put apricots into a saucepan and bring to a boil with lemon juice, salt and 1 cup water. Simmer, covered, 5 minutes, then drain, reserving the liquid. When cool enough to handle, cut each apricot half into 3 or 4 pieces.

Mix apricots with the rest of the ingredients except lamb. Add enough of the reserved apricot liquid to bring to the consistency of a spread.

Open out the leg of lamb and spread the apricot stuffing evenly over the inside. Then roll up the lamb and tie well with kitchen twine. Wrap rolled lamb *with* its bones around it in a tight package of heavy-duty foil. Refrigerate overnight.

Two hours before cooking time remove from refrigerator. Do not unwrap. Put lamb package in a shallow baking pan in a preheated 375° oven and roast, allowing 35 minutes per pound of lamb (weighed without bones).

Remove from oven 30 minutes before the end of cooking time. Raise oven heat to 400°. Unwrap lamb, discard bones, and return lamb to pan. Put back in oven 30 minutes to brown. Let stand 20 minutes before carving.
Serves 8.

Spinach Ring with Onions

6   10-ounce packages frozen
    chopped spinach
1   tablespoon butter
1   large onion, finely chopped
¼   teaspoon freshly ground black
    pepper
½   teaspoon salt
⅛   teaspoon nutmeg
½   cup grated Swiss cheese
1   cup milk, scalded
1   tablespoon beef extract
4   eggs, lightly beaten
1   20-ounce package frozen tiny
    white onions, thawed
2   tablespoons water
1   tablespoon butter

Cook frozen chopped spinach according to package directions. Drain very well and set aside to cool.

Melt the butter in a Teflon-lined pan, add the chopped onion, and sauté until limp. Put the cooled, well-drained spinach into a large bowl. Add the sautéed onion, pepper, salt, nutmeg and grated cheese.

Put milk and extract in a saucepan; heat, uncovered, just to scalding point. Remove from heat. Lightly beat the eggs in a cup. Slowly stir a spoonful or two of the hot milk into the beaten eggs. Then slowly add the egg mixture to the hot milk in the saucepan, stirring constantly until all is blended in.

Pour milk-and-egg mixture into the spinach bowl and mix well.

Lightly oil an 8-cup ring mold. Pour the spinach mixture into the mold and place it in a pan of hot water in a preheated 325° oven. Bake 35 or 40 minutes, or until a silver knife put in the center comes out clean. Remove from oven and allow to sit 5 minutes, then unmold (as directed on page 39) onto serving dish.

To make onion filling, place thawed onions with the rest of the ingredients in a large skillet. Cover and bring to a boil over medium heat. Lower the flame and continue cooking gently 5 minutes. Remove cover and cook for another few minutes until liquid evaporates. Place onions in center of spinach ring, and serve.

Serves 8.

Rabbit Food

I serve Rabbit Food in cut-glass dishes that belonged to my grandmother. Conventional salad often goes back to the kitchen untasted, but the relish dishes are emptied rapidly.

3 carrots, made into curls
8-ounce can pitted black olives
2 bunches radishes
1-pint box cherry tomatoes

Clean and prepare vegetables the day before and keep in plastic bags in the refrigerator until time to set them out.

Serves 8.

Lemon Ice Box Charlotte

12 ladyfingers, split
¾ cup orange juice
2-ounce package (2 envelopes)
    calorie-reduced lemon gelatin
2   cups boiling water
¼ cup lemon juice
2   egg whites
Pinch cream of tartar
2   tablespoons superfine sugar
1   teaspoon vanilla
2   cups calorie-reduced nondairy
    whipped topping

Sprinkle split ladyfingers with ¼ cup of the orange juice. Line a charlotte mold (or a small spring form pan) with the soaked ladyfingers, curved sides against the mold, cutting them to fit neatly in the bottom and around edges. (The ladyfingers must not be too moist or they will disintegrate; and if they are too dry, they won't adhere to the mold.)
Dissolve the lemon gelatin in the boiling water. Add the remaining ½ cup of orange juice and the lemon juice. Chill to the consistency of unbeaten egg white.

Beat egg whites with cream of tartar until soft peaks form. Add sugar a little at a time, with vanilla, beating until egg whites are stiff. Fold the egg whites and one cup of the whipped topping into the chilled gelatin mixture.

Pour the gelatin mixture into the lined charlotte mold and refrigerate, covered with plastic wrap, until firm.

At serving time, run a small sharp knife around the edges of the charlotte mold, place a chilled serving plate on top of the mold, and invert. (Or run the knife around the edges of the spring form before releasing sides.) Pass a small bowl with the remaining whipped topping.

Serves 8.

Fourth of July Party for Eight

Gazpacho
Salmon Steaks with Cucumber Sauce
Eggplant Farcie
Red, White and Blue Dessert

This is a nice menu to have before you go to see the fireworks. You can even make your own pyrotechnics if you can find some sparklers to stick in the dessert. If the thermometer soars, have the salmon cold. If the weather is reasonable and not seasonable serve it hot. I have a blue-and-white checkered cloth and I use red geraniums for a centerpiece. Put a few of George M. Cohan's songs on the hi-fi and you're off!

Gazpacho

Of all the dozens of gazpacho recipes I have tried, this is the simplest, easiest and most delicious.

8 large, ripe tomatoes, peeled, seeded and diced
1 medium onion, minced
2 large green peppers, finely chopped
3 garlic cloves, pressed
3 cups tomato juice
¼ cup wine vinegar
3 tablespoons salad oil
1 tablespoon salt
½ teaspoon freshly ground black pepper
4 teaspoons dry sherry
½ cup calorie-reduced sour cream

Mix all ingredients except sour cream and refrigerate. Serve in cream soup bowls with a blob (1 teaspoonful) of sour cream on each. Serves 8.

Salmon Steaks with Cucumber Sauce

4 lemons
8 salmon steaks, ¾- to 1-inch thick
Salt and pepper to taste
2 cucumbers, peeled, scored and sliced thin
1¼ cups calorie-reduced sour cream
1 teaspoon salt
¼ teaspoon freshly ground black pepper
2 tablespoons lemon juice
3 tablespoons fresh dill, finely chopped (or chopped chives)
2 tablespoons onion, finely minced

About an hour before cooking time squeeze half a lemon over each salmon steak, season with salt and pepper, and let remain at room temperature. When ready, broil about 3 inches from the heat approximately 6 minutes per side.

To make cucumber sauce, mix all remaining ingredients, place in a glass bowl, and chill well before serving. Pass with the salmon, or serve in little side dishes. Serves 8.

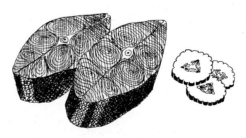

Eggplant Farcie

You can prepare this in the cool of the morning and reheat just before serving time.

4 eggplants, about 6 inches long, halved
Salt and pepper to taste
2 tablespoons butter
3 medium onions, finely chopped
½ cup bread crumbs
¼ cup chopped parsley
2 tablespoons grated Parmesan cheese

The eggplant shells are used to hold the stuffing. Place each eggplant half on a flat surface and cut a thin slice off the bottom of each, so it will sit flat. Scoop out the inside, leaving a ½-inch shell. Put the eggplant pulp in a saucepan, with water to cover, and boil 15 minutes, lid on. Drain well and mash. Season with salt and pepper.

Melt butter in a Teflon pan and sauté chopped onion until it is just golden. Mix sautéed onion with mashed eggplant (stir in a few of the bread crumbs if the mixture looks too thin).

Place the eggplant mixture in the shells. Put the filled shells on a cookie sheet. Sprinkle tops with bread crumbs, chopped parsley, and grated Parmesan. You can hold the shells in the refrigerator at this point.

Just before serving time put into a preheated 375° oven and bake 15 minutes, until brown and bubbling. Transfer Eggplant Farcie to heated platter and serve at once.

Serves 8.

Red, White and Blue Dessert

2-ounce package (2 envelopes) calorie-reduced strawberry gelatin
4 cups boiling water
2 pints fresh strawberries
2-ounce package (2 envelopes) calorie-reduced lemon gelatin
4 cups boiling water
2 pints blueberries
1 pint vanilla ice milk
Sparklers (optional)

Make strawberry gelatin as directed on package, using 4 cups boiling water. Place in a bowl (not metal) in refrigerator to chill. When it is nearly set, but still stirrable, fold in fresh strawberries. Pour into a wet 8-cup ring mold and return to refrigerator to harden.

Make lemon gelatin as directed on package, using 4 cups boiling water. Place in a bowl (not metal) in refrigerator to chill. When it is nearly set, but still stirrable, mix in the blueberries. Keep at room temperature so that it will maintain its fluidity. As soon as the strawberry mixture is set, pour the blueberry mixture in the ring mold on top of it. Return to refrigerator to chill until serving time.

At serving time unmold (as directed on page 117) onto a white serving plate and fill the center with vanilla ice milk. If you wish, place sparklers in the ice milk and light them. Bear proudly to the table, singing "I'm a Yankee Doodle Dandy" or any other appropriate song.

Serves 8.

A Thanksgiving Feast for Eight

Relish Tray
Roast Turkey
Marco Polo Dressing
Hubbard Squash
Scalloped Oysters Williamsburg
Brussels Sprouts
Whole Cranberry Sauce
Spiced Cranberry Jelly
Pumpkin Soufflé

The bounty that appears on our tables the last Thursday in November is the most deeply cherished tradition of our many holidays. Although there are regional and ethnic variations in different parts of the country, the main theme is similar. Turkey with all the "fixin's"—several kinds of potatoes, vegetables, relishes, several pies, nuts and fruit, plus rolls and butter, amounts to a vast amount of highly caloric food. Over the years I have cut down on the overall richness of the Thanksgiving menu served at our house. No one has seemed to notice.

Relish Tray

The relish tray can be passed in the living room if you are serving cocktails before dinner. If not, place it on the table and it can be passed around as the host is carving.

All the vegetables for the relish tray can be prepared in advance, held in the refrigerator in covered containers, and arranged on plate or tray just before serving.

1 recipe Oil and Vinegar Dressing
    (page 189)
10-ounce package frozen asparagus
    spears
1 recipe Beets Vinaigrette
    (page 27)
1 recipe Cucumbers à la Dansk
    (page 152)
Pint box cherry tomatoes

Make the Oil and Vinegar Dressing. Cook asparagus according to package directions, drain well, and pat dry with paper towels. Put in flat, rimmed dish and pour the dressing over it. Cover with plastic wrap and marinate overnight in the refrigerator.

Make Beets Vinaigrette.

Make Cucumbers à la Dansk.

Wash the cherry tomatoes and pat dry with paper towels.

At serving time, drain all vegetables and arrange prettily on a serving plate.

Serves 8.

Roast Turkey

There is a wealth of turkeys available in this country today—small, medium, and large; fresh, fresh-frozen, fresh-chilled, ready-to-cook, frozen self-basting, stuffed or unstuffed; frozen uncooked turkey rolls, or turkey roasts, of white meat or dark, or both; turkey halves, turkey quarters, turkey parts—steaks, thighs, wings, drumsticks, breast, and giblets. All I can say is, follow the printed directions on whatever package you bring home.

Or try my method for roasting turkey, with delicious Marco Polo Dressing.

I like to roast turkey uncovered and baste with a mixture of white wine and turkey broth.

8- to 12-pound turkey
1 onion
1 stalk celery
A little salt
1 to 2 cups (or more) dry white
    wine
Olive oil
Coarse salt
Freshly ground black pepper

For the basting liquid, put turkey neck in a saucepan with an onion and a celery stalk and water to cover; simmer, lid on, for 1 hour. Strain broth into a measuring cup and add an equal amount of dry white wine. Return to saucepan and place on back of stove.

Make the Marco Polo Dressing.

Spoon it loosely into the turkey, trussing it so wings and legs lie close to the body. Rub all over with a little olive oil—not enough to drip, just the lightest coat. Now rub lightly with coarse salt and pepper. Place on its *side* in an open roaster and put into a preheated 350° oven.

For timing, see table. Roast on its side for one third of the time, turn to the other side for the next third, then turn breast up to brown until the end. Baste often with the basting liquid, which will soon mix with the turkey's own drippings. (Some people prefer to cover the bird tightly with foil and uncover to brown only for the last 45 minutes of cooking. In this case, the turkey stays breast up the whole time.)

Whichever method you use, the best way to test for doneness is to insert a meat thermometer in the thickest part of the thigh (not touching bone). When the temperature is 180° to 185° the turkey is done. But you should take the bird out of the oven when the thermometer registers 175°—let it stand at room temperature for 30 minutes before carving, by which time the internal temperature will have risen to 185°.

Spoon off the fat in the roasting pan and deglaze all those good brown crusty bits with a little hot vegetable juice or white wine. This pan gravy does not resemble ordinary flour gravy, but to my mind the plain turkey juices are infinitely more delicious, and not as fattening, either.

Serves 8 or more.

Time Chart for Roasting a Whole Stuffed Turkey at 350°

Ready-to-Cook Weight	Total Roasting Time
6 to 8 pounds	2 to 2½ hours
8 to 12 pounds	2½ to 3 hours
12 to 16 pounds	3 to 3¾ hours
16 to 20 pounds	3¾ to 4½ hours
20 to 24 pounds	5½ to 6½ hours

Marco Polo Dressing

You should make turkey dressing shortly before stuffing and roasting the turkey, as dressing tends to be a good culture medium for harmful bacteria.

4 large square matzos, crumbled into 1-inch pieces (or 6 slices diet bread)
2 cups warm water
2 tablespoons butter
1 large onion, finely chopped
1 cup celery, with leaves, chopped
2 cloves garlic, pressed
1 package "brown and serve" sausages, link or patty
16-ounce can bean sprouts, drained and rinsed
5-ounce can water chestnuts, drained and diced
5-ounce can bamboo shoots drained and rinsed
1 tablespoon poultry seasoning
½ teaspoon salt
¼ teaspoon pepper
A pinch of thyme
A pinch of marjoram
A pinch of tarragon
¼ cup orange juice
2 eggs, lightly beaten

Place crumbled matzos in bowl, cover with warm water, drain at once and squeeze dry. Melt 1 tablespoon of the butter in a Teflon pan, add drained matzos, and sauté until brown. Remove from heat and set aside.

Heat the remaining tablespoon of butter in the same pan, add onion, celery, and garlic, and sauté until golden brown.

Cut sausages in pieces, or crumble patties. Put under the broiler for about 5 minutes to brown. Then drain sausage on paper towels to remove excess fat.

In a large bowl combine browned sausage meat, matzos, onion, celery and garlic. Add drained bean sprouts, water chestnuts and bamboo shoots, poultry seasoning, salt, pepper and herbs. Pour in orange juice and stir in beaten eggs. Mix well. Refrigerate until roasting time.

Spoon lightly into turkey cavities and lace openings with skewers and kitchen twine.

Makes enough to stuff a 10-pound turkey.

(For a larger bird, 12 to 15 pounds, add 2 matzos and another 5-ounce can of bamboo shoots.)

Hubbard Squash

Oh, bless the man who decided to freeze Hubbard squash! What a lot of work he has saved us all. When you prepare the squash in this manner you never miss the butter!

4 10-ounce packages frozen squash
1 onion, finely chopped
Salt and pepper to taste

Let squash defrost at room temperature. Chop onion and mix well with thawed squash; add salt and pepper to taste. Place in a covered 1-quart casserole.

The minute you take the turkey out of the oven, raise the temperature to 400° and immediately put in the Hubbard squash (and the scalloped oysters) to bake for 30 minutes.

Serves 8.

Scalloped Oysters Williamsburg

This can be made several weeks ahead and put in the freezer, or make it a day ahead and hold in refrigerator. In any case, bring to room temperature before baking. In our house it's not Thanksgiving without this traditional dish.

¼ cup butter
¼ cup flour
1½ tablespoons paprika
Salt and pepper to taste
Dash of cayenne (optional)
1   onion, finely chopped
½ green pepper, finely chopped
½ clove garlic, pressed
1   quart of oysters, opened
1   teaspoon lemon juice
1   tablespoon Worcestershire sauce
¼ cup cracker crumbs

Melt butter, add flour, and cook 5 minutes, or until light brown, stirring constantly. Add paprika, salt, pepper and cayenne. Cook 3 minutes. Add onion, green pepper and garlic and cook over lowered heat 5 minutes. Remove from fire.

Pick over oysters, put into a saucepan, and heat in their own juice just until hot—do not cook. Combine with the onion and green pepper mixture, and add lemon juice and Worcestershire sauce.

Pour into a 1-quart baking dish and sprinkle top with cracker crumbs. (At this point you can freeze or refrigerate, tightly covered.)

As soon as the turkey comes out of the oven, raise temperature to 400° and put in the scalloped oysters (along with Hubbard squash) to bake for 30 minutes.

Serves 8.

Brussels Sprouts

You may use fresh brussels sprouts, but I have never seen any in my market as tiny as the little frozen ones.

4 10-ounce packages tiny frozen
    brussels sprouts
Salt and pepper
Chopped parsley

Cook the frozen brussels sprouts according to package directions, just until soft but not squashy, and still a beautiful green. Drain at once.

Serve in your best vegetable dish with some chopped parsley sprinkled on top.

Serves 8.

Whole Cranberry Sauce

This adds glitter and glow to your buffet table, as well as spice to the taste. There'll probably be some left to serve with your cold turkey.

4 cups uncooked cranberries
2 cups water
1 cup sugar
2 teaspoons grated orange peel

Wash and pick over cranberries.

Place water and sugar in a saucepan over low heat and stir until sugar is dissolved. Bring to a boil and simmer uncovered for 5 minutes. Add cranberries. Simmer very gently over low heat, without stirring, for about 5 minutes. Skim off any foam. Add grated orange peel. Pour into a 6-cup mold that has been rinsed with cold water, and chill until firm. Unmold as directed on page 117.

Serves 8.

Spiced Cranberry Jelly

4 cups cranberries
2 cups boiling water
1 cup sugar
1 piece stick cinnamon
2 whole cloves
¼ teaspoon salt

Wash and pick over cranberries. Place in a saucepan and cover with 2 cups boiling water. As soon as the cranberries come to a boil, put the lid on and boil for 3 or 4 minutes, or until the cranberries burst. At once put through a strainer. Stir in the sugar until dissolved. Add cinnamon, cloves and salt, return strained cranberry juices to pan, and boil, uncovered, for 5 minutes more.

Remove cinnamon stick and cloves. Pour into a wet 6-cup mold and chill until jellied. Unmold as directed on page 117.

Serves 8.

Pumpkin Soufflé

This can be made the day before. It has all the flavor and zing of pumpkin pie, and isn't nearly as fattening.

1½ cups mashed cooked pumpkin
    (canned will do nicely)
7   large eggs, slightly beaten
1½ cups evaporated skim milk
⅓   cup water
2   teaspoons vanilla extract
⅓   cup sugar
1   teaspoon ground cinnamon
¼   teaspoon ground ginger
½   teaspoon salt
12-ounce container calorie-reduced
    nondairy whipped topping

Combine all ingredients except whipped topping. Mix well. Turn into a 6-cup soufflé dish (or other straight-sided oven dish). Set in a pan of hot water in a preheated 350° oven and bake 1¼ hours, or until a silver knife inserted in the center comes out clean.

Chill before serving. A dish of whipped topping may be passed separately.

Serves 8.

CHAPTER NINE

Basic Calorie-reduced Recipes

*T*he following recipes are for things that no diet-conscious person should be without, either in the freezer or refrigerator. Some are for salad dressings, some are for fat-free bouillons, some are for sauces. Besides being healthy, many of them are economical. Water that vegetables have been cooked in should be saved as precious liquid and used in gravies, sauces and soups instead of plain water. (Vitamins present in vegetables go down the drain when you discard their cooking water.) And never throw away a bone! At least, not until you have wrung every vital drop from it.

Years ago, when all the family was still at home, my freezer contained things like a hindquarter of beef, eight loaves of bread, several gallons of ice cream. The picture is different today. There are little pint containers of chicken, beef, veal and vegetable bouillon; all fat-free. Chicken, veal and fish abound instead of all that beef. No ice cream, either—only a couple of pints of sherbet. I cook double amounts of stews and things like chop suey and pepper steak, remove all the fat that congeals when cold, then store half of the stew or whatever in the freezer until a quick meal is needed.

Calorie-reduced Mayonnaise

Barbara Gibbons, lecturer on creative low-calorie cooking, deserves the credit for inventing this excellent mayonnaise substitute. It not only tastes like mayonnaise, it looks like it. An added advantage is that it can be frozen. It keeps 10 to 12 days in the refrigerator in a screw-top jar. Best of all, there are only 16 calories per *tablespoon!* Keep it on hand, and you will not be tempted to reach for the real thing.

Note that this dressing cannot be used in any recipe that requires cooking; it will separate.

1 **cup part-skim ricotta cheese** (or calorie-reduced cottage cheese, or plain yogurt)
1 **hard-boiled egg, shelled and quartered**
½ **teaspoon dry mustard**
½ **teaspoon salt**
½ **teaspoon celery salt**

Put all ingredients in blender. Blend at high speed 1 minute. Pour into screw-top jar and refrigerate.

When the dressing is first made it is slightly more liquid than regular mayonnaise, but chilling in the refrigerator brings it to the right consistency.

Makes slightly more than 1 cup.

Herbed Dressing

This has so much flavor that no one will guess that the base of this dressing is your Calorie-reduced Mayonnaise.

1 **recipe Calorie-reduced Mayonnaise** (above)
4 **tablespoons cider vinegar**
2 **teaspoons onion juice**
3 **dashes Tabasco**
1 **teaspoon prepared mustard**
1 **teaspoon chili powder**
½ **teaspoon dried thyme**
½ **teaspoon dried marjoram**
1 **teaspoon salt**
¼ **teaspoon freshly ground black pepper**

Place all ingredients in an empty pint jar with a screw-type lid and shake well until mixed.

Makes about 1 cup.

Calorie-reduced Russian Dressing

2 recipes Calorie-reduced
    Mayonnaise (page 187)
5 tablespoons prepared horseradish
2 tablespoons mustard (Dijon type)
¼ cup chili sauce
¼ cup tomato catsup
½ teaspoon paprika
1 teaspoon salt
1 medium onion, grated
2 tablespoons vinegar
1 tablespoon lemon juice
⅛ teaspoon black pepper

Combine all ingredients and mix well together. Store in screw-top jar in refrigerator.

Makes 2½ to 3 cups.

Fruit Salad Dressing

This goes well with any kind of fruit salad, with or without cottage cheese.

½ recipe Calorie-reduced
    Mayonnaise (page 187)
4 tablespoons lemon juice
4 tablespoons orange juice
1 tablespoon honey
½ teaspoon celery seed

Put all ingredients into blender, and blend at high speed for 30 seconds.

Makes about 1 cup.

Sweet Coleslaw Dressing

Use to dress cabbage—red, white or Chinese.

¾ cup Calorie-reduced Mayonnaise
    (page 187)
¼ cup calorie-reduced nondairy
    whipped topping
½ teaspoon celery seed
¼ teaspoon salt

¼ teaspoon white pepper

Combine all ingredients and mix well.

Makes 1 cup.

Blue Cheese Dressing

This is a smooth, creamy dressing.

⅓ cup skim milk
1 cup calorie-reduced cottage
    cheese
½ cup blue cheese
1 teaspoon seasoned salt
2 tablespoons lemon juice

Place all ingredients in blender and blend at high speed 2 minutes, until dressing is smooth.
    Makes about 2 cups.

Oil and Lemon Dressing

Nothing ersatz in this dressing, just carefully worked-out proportions to make a tart, lemony dressing. When you apply it to the greens, toss, toss, toss. This is valuable stuff and it has to go a long way. Be sure to toss the salad for at least 30 seconds—watch the clock, or get one of the children to count.

2 tablespoons salad oil (any kind)
4 tablespoons lemon juice
2 tablespoons chopped parsley
¼ teaspoon dry mustard
¼ teaspoon salt
A good grating of black pepper

Combine all the ingredients in a blender and blend at high speed for 30 seconds.
    Makes 6 tablespoons—that is, 1 tablespoon per serving for 6.

Oil and Vinegar Dressing

This is the basis of any type of vinaigrette dressing. It is excellent on asparagus, broccoli, and green beans.

4 tablespoons olive oil
1 tablespoon vinegar
¼ teaspoon prepared mustard
½ teaspoon salt
¼ teaspoon freshly ground black
    pepper
1 tablespoon mixed chopped
    parsley, chives, and chervil

Combine all ingredients in a small bowl and beat well with a fork.
    Makes 6 tablespoons—that is, 1 tablespoon per serving for 6.
Variation:
    For garlic dressing, add 1 clove of garlic, pressed, to the ingredients above.

Tomato Dressing

This is very tangy, and you do not miss the oil. Goes very well with cottage cheese and tomatoes, string beans or watercress.

3 tablespoons tomato sauce
2 tablespoons tarragon vinegar
6-ounce package garlic-cheese salad
    dressing mix
4 tablespoons ice water

Combine everything in a bottle and shake well.
Makes ½ cup.

Barbecue Sauce

1 cup catsup
2 cups dry red wine
1 cup onion, finely chopped
1 cup green pepper, finely chopped
1 cup celery, finely chopped
2 tablespoons prepared mustard
3 tablespoons calorie-reduced
    maple syrup
1 teaspoon garlic powder

½ teaspoon oregano

Combine all ingredients in a saucepan. Bring to a boil, lower heat, and cook, uncovered, to desired consistency, stirring occasionally. This takes from 45 minutes to an hour—you want it thickened, but not stiff.
Makes about 6 cups.

Zesty Dip

1 recipe Calorie-reduced
    Mayonnaise (page 187)
½ cup chili sauce
1 clove garlic, pressed
Dash Tabasco
½ teaspoon lime juice

1 tablespoon horseradish

Mix all ingredients together in a small bowl. Refrigerate until needed.
Makes 1½ cups.

Sour Cream Dip

16-ounce container calorie-reduced
    sour cream
½ 2¾-ounce package (1 envelope)
    onion soup mix
2 cloves garlic, pressed
Skim milk (if needed to moisten)

If the sour cream seems a little

stiff, stir well to loosen it up. Add the rest of the ingredients and mix well. (If it is too thick, moisten with a spoonful or two of skim milk.) Put into a bowl and chill until serving time.
Makes about 2 cups.

American-French Dressing

2 teaspoons salt
½ teaspoon freshly ground black
    pepper
1 teaspoon sugar
1 teaspoon celery seed
3 tablespoons olive oil
1 tablespoon red wine vinegar

¼ cup tomato juice

Place everything in the blender. Blend at high speed 30 seconds.

Makes about ½ cup—that is, a little more than 1 tablespoon per serving for 6.

Calorie-reduced Dip for Vegetables

Use as a dip for raw vegetables such as cauliflower, carrots, tender baby string beans, cucumber strips, and zucchini strips.

1 teaspoon Worcestershire sauce
Dash of Tabasco
6 ounces calorie-reduced cottage
    cheese
¼ cup canned pimientos (water-
    packed)
¼ teaspoon salt
¼ teaspoon celery salt

1 clove garlic

Place all ingredients in blender and blend at high speed until smooth, about 2 minutes.

Put into a bowl and chill until serving time.

Makes about 1 cup.

Skinny Shake

This is another of Barbara Gibbons' calorie-savers, an excellent coating for chicken, fish, and cutlets that are baked in the oven instead of fried. Make up a batch and keep in a screw-top jar in the refrigerator. It keeps three or four weeks. Take out as much as you need, coat your food, and pour the unused portion back in the jar.

16-ounce package bread crumbs
½ cup salad oil
Seasonings to taste—¼ teaspoon of
    any or all of the following:
    onion salt, paprika, pepper, garlic
    powder, celery seeds, instant
    bouillon
Pinch of any or all of the following:
    thyme, marjoram, savory, poultry
    seasoning, parsley

Empty bread crumbs into a bowl and stir in salad oil with fork or pastry blender. Add seasonings to taste, and mix well.

Pour into a screw-top jar and keep tightly closed in the refrigerator.

Makes 4 cups of crumbs (½ cup coats 2½ pounds cut-up chicken).

Calorie-reduced Spaghetti Sauce

This is a wonderful sauce to have on hand—a spoonful will add a lot of zip to many dishes as well as to spaghetti.

16-ounce can Italian plum tomatoes
2 tablespoons onion, chopped
1 clove garlic, pressed
1 tablespoon parsley, chopped
1 tablespoon instant beef bouillon powder
1 teaspoon fresh basil (or ½ teaspoon dried)
½ teaspoon oregano
1 teaspoon salt
½ teaspoon freshly ground black pepper
½ pound mushrooms, sliced (or 8-ounce can sliced mushrooms (optional)

Put the tomatoes with their juice through a sieve to remove seeds and form a pulp. Place in a saucepan with all the other ingredients and bring to a boil. Lower heat and simmer gently, partly covered, for about 40 minutes. Stir occasionally so it will not stick. (Mushrooms can be added to this if your family likes them.)

Makes about 3 cups.

Quick Fat-free Bouillons

There are four different ways you can approach the quick fat-free bouillon subject. All of these products are perfectly acceptable for use in the recipes in this book—if you don't want to spend the time making from scratch your beef, chicken or vegetable bouillons.

1. **Canned consommé:** contains gelatin, may be eaten chilled and jelled without any further additions. It is perfectly fat-free.

2. **Canned bouillon:** beef bouillon is fat-free, not so chicken. So chill the can of chicken bouillon in the refrigerator and when you open it, carefully remove the layer of fat that congeals on top.

3. **Instant bouillon powder:** very handy, comes in 3 flavors—beef, chicken and vegetable. Reconstitute with hot water. Fat-free.

4. **Bouillon cubes:** these have a trace of fat and take a little longer to reconstitute into broth. Often excessively salty.

There is a fifth method, but you can't call it quick, because it takes time. Make your own, and keep it on hand in your freezer. My New England ancestors make me feel uncomfortable about throwing out a chicken carcass or some roast beef bones. Here, following, is what I do with them.

Fat-free Beef Bouillon

4 pounds beef shin, with bones
3 veal bones
1 tablespoon coarse salt
4 quarts water
½ cup onions, coarsely chopped
1 leek, chopped
½ cup parsley, chopped
3 carrots, coarsely chopped
1 cup celery with leaves, coarsely
   chopped
6 peppercorns

Leave the meat whole, do not cut up. Place the meat, veal bones and salt in a large kettle, cover with 4 quarts of water, and bring to a boil. Skim the scum that forms on top with a slotted spoon. Meanwhile, chop the vegetables and add them to the boiling stock along with the peppercorns. Cover and simmer 2 or 3 hours. Drain through a sieve. You can use the meat as boiled beef for dinner (waste not, want not). Discard vegetables.

Wash and dry the kettle well. Replace the strained liquid in the kettle and simmer, uncovered, for 1¼ hours or more, until reduced to 2 quarts. Strain into a bowl through 2 layers of wet cheesecloth. Refrigerate. When all fat is congealed on top, remove it. Store in 1-pint containers in freezer. Keeps for months.

Makes 4 pints.

Fat-free Chicken Bouillon

Never throw out a chicken carcass. You can use it to make two cups of chicken bouillon. Save chicken backs and necks in a plastic bag in the freezer until you have enough to make it worthwhile to make soup. I use a pressure cooker because it takes so little time, but it isn't necessary.

4- to 5-pound stewing hen (or 3
   pounds backs and wings, or 2
   fryers or broilers)
2 onions, coarsely chopped
2 celery stalks with leaves, coarsely
   chopped
1 tablespoon coarse salt
3 quarts water

Place the chicken, whole or cut up, whichever you are using, in a large kettle. Add onions, celery, salt, and water. Bring to a boil. Skim any scum that rises to the top with a slotted spoon. Simmer 2 or 3 hours. (Fryers will be done long before an old hen has cooked tender, so check on tenderness after about an hour.)

If you are using fowl, remove the bird when the breast is tender and cut the entire breast off the carcass. Return the carcass to the kettle and continue cooking. The breast meat may be used for salad, hash, cold chicken, or Chicken Divine (page 141).

Strain the chicken broth through 2 layers of wet cheesecloth into a bowl. Refrigerate until cold and all fat has congealed on top. Remove every speck of fat.

You can store the bouillon in 8-ounce containers in your freezer.

Makes 3 pints.

Fat-free Vegetable Bouillon

Vegetable bouillon can be the basis for an aspic salad, or it can be served as hot bouillon for an appetizer. You can also use it without straining, as a very pleasant vegetable soup, in which case you can add string beans or peas, if you have some handy. It fills you up without filling you out.

½ cup onions, chopped
½ cup cabbage, chopped
2 cups celery, with leaves, chopped
½ cup carrots, chopped
½ cup turnips, chopped (optional)
1 teaspoon instant vegetable
    bouillon powder
¼ cup hot water
4 cups water
2 cups tomato juice
2 teaspoons salt
6 peppercorns

Place the chopped vegetables in a soup kettle. Dissolve the vegetable extract in hot water and add to the kettle with the 4 cups water and the tomato juice. Simmer, covered, for an hour or so. Add salt and peppercorns.

Remove cover and simmer for another half hour. Strain and store in 1-pint containers in your freezer.

Makes 3 pints.

Calorie-reduced White Sauce

White sauce was the first thing I learned to cook in 7th-grade cooking class. It is still a good thing to know, and recently I learned to make one that is less calorie-laden.

These are directions for medium white sauce. To increase the thickness, increase the butter and flour; everything else remains the same.

1 cup water
¼ cup dry skim milk powder
2 tablespoons flour
¼ teaspoon salt
2 tablespoons butter

Pour water in saucepan, add milk powder, flour and salt and beat with a wire whisk until smooth. Add butter, put over low heat, and cook, stirring constantly, until thickened (6 or 7 minutes).

Makes 1 cup.

Variations:

Cheese sauce: add ½ cup grated cheese and stir in until it melts.

Curry sauce: add ½ teaspoon curry powder.

Egg sauce: add 1 or 2 chopped hard-cooked eggs to the thickened sauce.

Herb sauce: Sauté 2 teaspoons chopped chives and 2 teaspoons chopped parsley in the butter before adding to milk mixture. Then add a pinch each of marjoram and thyme.

Horseradish sauce: add ⅓ cup drained prepared horseradish to the thickened sauce.

Mushroom sauce: add ¼ teaspoon Worcestershire sauce and ½ cup chopped cooked mushrooms to the thickened sauce.

Mustard sauce: stir 2 teaspoons prepared mustard into the thickened sauce.

Pickle sauce: add 3 tablespoons chopped pickles and 1 teaspoon salt to the thickened sauce.

Pimiento sauce: add 2 tablespoons chopped pimiento and a dash of freshly ground black pepper to the thickened sauce.

Appendix

The products listed here are distributed country-wide, but there are many good low-calorie food items that are only to be found locally. Some calorie-reduced foods taste better than others, and these are the ones I like and generally use. Always try any new item before serving it to your unsuspecting guests, because although many are delicious, occasionally you will find an off-brand that tastes really ghastly.

Bouillons: any canned beef or chicken bouillon; all instant bouillons and bouillon cubes

Chocolate syrup: Diet Delight

Coarse salt: usually available as boxed kosher salt

Concentrated seasoning bases or extracts:
beef-flavored: Bovril
vegetarian beef-flavored: Savita
chicken-flavored: McCormick

Fruit and fruit juices (canned): Diet Delight; Featherweight; Diet Mott's; Ocean Spray Low Calorie

Gelatin:
sweet desserts: D-Zerta; Shimmer
unsweetened: Knox

Jams, jellies, and preserves: Dia-mel; Polaner's New-Jam

Maple syrup: Cary's Low-calorie Maple Syrup

Margarine: Diet Imperial

Mayonnaise: Mayo 7 (can be used for cooking)

Milk products:
cottage cheese: Sealtest Light n' Lively
skim milk: dry powdered: Alba; Carnation; Pet
evaporated (canned): Borden's; Whitehouse (A & P)
liquid: all dairies
sour cream: check local brands
yogurt: Borden's; Breakstone; Sealtest Light n' Lively

Raspberry syrup: No-Cal Raspberry Syrup

Puddings: D-Zerta (vanilla and chocolate)

Soups: Claybourne's Diet Soups

Index